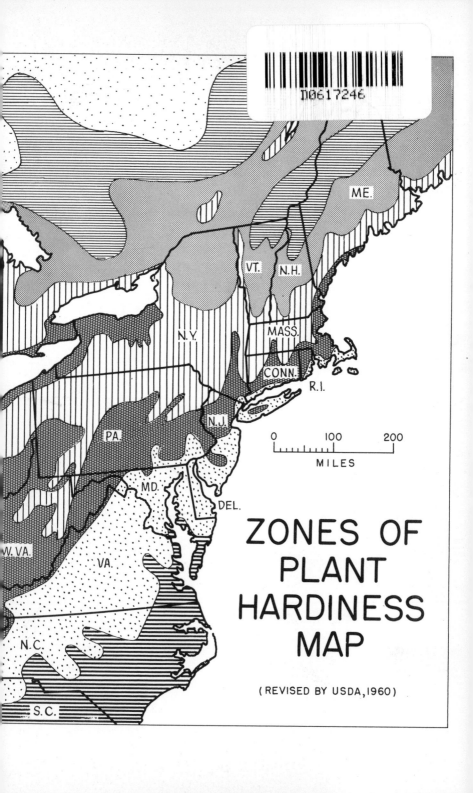

ZONES OF PLANT HARDINESS MAP

(REVISED BY USDA, 1960)

ESPALIERS

AND VINES

FOR THE

HOME GARDENER

Espaliers and Vines
for the Home Gardener

by

Harold O. Perkins

Drawings by Kathleen Bourke

D. VAN NOSTRAND COMPANY, INC.

Princeton, New Jersey

Toronto
New york
London

D. VAN NOSTRAND COMPANY, INC.
120 Alexander St., Princeton, New Jersey (*Principal office*)
24 West 40 Street, New York 18, New York

D. Van Nostrand Company, Ltd.
358, Kensington High Street, London, W.14, England

D. Van Nostrand Company (Canada), Ltd.
25 Hollinger Road, Toronto 16, Canada

PRINTED IN THE UNITED STATES OF AMERICA

TO MARY GWENDOLYN

With Thanks

Many people have helped me write this book. Special thanks go to Henry Leuthardt, Sr., and his son Henry, of Port Chester, New York, for assisting me with the chapter on espalier fruit trees; to Everett A. Piester, retired Superintendent of Parks, Hartford, Connecticut, and formerly in charge of that city's Elizabeth Park Rose Garden, for his help on climbing roses; to Dr. Milton Savos, Extension Entomologist, College of Agriculture of the University of Connecticut, for up-to-the-minute information on pest control; and to Dr. Henry T. Skinner, National Arboretum, Washington, D.C., who was helpful in many ways, and particularly for his assistance in assigning zone numbers to the plants described, so that they would conform to the 1960 United States Department of Agriculture Plant Hardiness Zone Map.

In addition, I give recognition to the authors of the books to which I turned most frequently for reference: to Donald Wyman for his *Shrubs and Vines for American Gardens* and *Trees for American Gardens*; to Stanley B. Whitehead for *Fruit from Trained Trees*; to Alfred Rehder for his *Manual of Cultivated Trees and Shrubs*; to W. J. Bean for his *Trees and Shrubs Hardy in the British Isles*; and to Florence Bell Robinson for her *Useful Trees and Shrubs*.

My appreciation goes to the Kansas City firm of McDonald/Bourke for helping me with the manuscript in its final stages—to Kathleen Bourke for the artwork, and to Elvin

McDonald for editorial assistance. And finally, my deepest gratitude to the librarians, who seem always to know where to find the answers, and to the longest-suffering of them all, my wife—typist, plodder, and prodder extraordinary.

Harold O. Perkins

Storrs, Connecticut
January, 1964

As the Twig Is Bent

THE TRAINING OF PLANTS is a major—and absorbing—avocation for today's home gardener, and there are many plants that are rewarding to work with. Espaliers and vines have been grouped together in this book because training methods for them are similar. Other popular ways of shaping and controlling plant growth include oriental pruning, topiary or sculpturing, bonsai or dwarfing, the pleaching of trees, the clipping of hedges, and the training of normally bushy plants to standard or tree forms.

THE MEANING OF "ESPALIER"

Espalier is a French word derived from the Italian *spalliera*, something to rest the *spalla* (shoulder) against. It came into the English language in the seventeenth century, and referred originally to the trellis or frame upon which a plant was trained. Today we have given the word two more meanings, both in common usage. "Espalier" may describe any plant trained flat in one plane—a two-dimensional tree or shrub, as it were, with height and width, but almost no depth. "Espalier" may be used also as a verb to describe the technique of training a plant to this flat plane. The pronunciation, according to *Webster's New World Dictionary*, is simply "ess-PAL-yer," or "ess-PAL-yerd."

Among the first to train trees in this way were the Romans, who espaliered fruit trees against their walls. The practice was later adopted by the people of central Europe and England, where skilled gardeners developed it to a fine degree. In the cool and cloudy weather of England, fruit trees were often placed on the south side of a wall to take advantage of reflected heat. Espaliers have also played an important role in elaborately designed kitchen gardens, where they were used against a wall or along a central path to serve as background, or to screen one area from another. In Spain, orange trees were espaliered in the courtyards, where their dark, glossy foliage, flowers and fruit showed to good advantage, yet needed little ground space.

In these older gardens of Europe, the espalier training of fruit trees was done only by persons of great skill. They used formal patterns, and their methods were passed down from one generation to another. It was from these gardeners that we obtained the basic espalier patterns described and illustrated in Chapter 2. In the past, such intricate schemes were developed for espaliers that names could even be spelled with them. Today's smaller gardens need espaliers trained into simple formal patterns or informal designs that do not require the attention of a trained gardener. Fortunately, selected ornamental shrubs and small trees answer this need and provide pleasing solutions to many a landscape problem.

VINES FOR TODAY

Vines used in the outdoor garden have many espalier characteristics. Basically, they are plants trained in one plane, either vertical or horizontal. For example, a grapevine may be trained upward on a trellis, or it may be trained vertically until it reaches the top of an arbor or eggcrate type of framework over an outdoor living area, there to spread out in a horizontal plane to provide dappled shade.

Vines, like espaliers, are space-savers. Many ways of using them are discussed in Chapters 9 and 10; the vines included have been selected with the small gardens of today in mind.

Four important factors were considered in choosing each tree, shrub and vine described in this book. The first consideration was its value in landscape design. Next its mature size was considered; that is, its ability to create a desired effect in the landscape without taking space away from any valuable outdoor living area. The third factor was its possible use in climate modification, primarily to shade or screen some portion of the landscape. The fourth consideration was fruit production.

There may be nothing new under the sun, but if an ancient practice is revived with a fresh approach, it becomes to all intents and purposes an original venture. When such a revival is not a mere passing novelty, but something of value that could become an important and permanent part of our present-day lives, we have good reason to take notice. Hence, this book was written—to tell how to use, plant and train espaliers and vines in decorative ways.

Contents

Illustrations

DRAWINGS

FIGURE

Part 1

Espaliers for the Home Garden

Use and Basic Patterns for Espaliers

Residential and business structures of today are often characterized by expanses of unadorned wall. This concept of functional design pleases architect and builder, but it presents the gardener with problems—or opportunities, depending on his outlook. Certainly a blank wall is not likely to be a thing of beauty, and may even be unsightly, as in the exposed concrete foundations of suburbia's split-level homes.

Is a foundation planting the answer? Sometimes, yes, but the original idea, to soften the lines of the house, has been grossly abused. The foundation plantings of most buildings quickly grow out of bounds. Either they overpower and hide good architectural lines, or they become so massive that the shrubs have to be sheared back into unnatural forms.

Espaliered plants offer a nearly perfect solution to problems of bare walls and exposed foundations. The optimistic gardener will consider these surfaces as canvases against which he can create pleasing compositions of plant materials. Essentially, then, espaliering makes certain shrubs and trees suitable for today's gardens where space would not permit them to develop naturally.

Espaliers display all of the finer details of plants—line of stem, texture of bark and subtle variations in the color and

3

PYRACANTHA (FIRETHORN) ESPALIERED AS AN INFORMAL FAN ON A HOUSE WALL GIVES GREEN FOLIAGE ALL YEAR, WHITE FLOWERS IN SPRING, AND BRIGHT ORANGE BERRIES THROUGH FALL AND EARLY WINTER, YET TAKES ALMOST NO GROUND SPACE.   (Max Tatch)

shape of leaf, flower and fruit. In addition, espaliers take up a minimum of ground space. Today, more than ever, areas left for planting near the house are likely to be narrow, since extensive paving may be used for an outdoor living area, a

PEARS TRAINED BY THE PALMETTE VERRIER SYSTEM AGAINST SIDE OF HOUSE SERVE AS OBJECTS OF ART BY TERRACE AND PROVIDE A FRUIT CROP BESIDES.   (*Paul E. Genereux*)

driveway or a service yard. There are espaliers adaptable to any space, whether it is high or low, narrow or wide.

Simple espaliers may be used to provide background for a garden of flowers or vegetables, a paved terrace, a lawn or a play area. Espaliers are ideal as privacy screens. Several may be combined as a baffle to afford more privacy for a terrace or patio, at the same time allowing foot traffic to move through, perhaps to a flower garden beyond, an expanse of lawn or the children's play yard.

Espaliers make ideal focal points for terraces and patios, for garage panels, for fences or beside garden paths. On wall or fence, they may take the place of rampant vines or massive shrubbery.

When espaliers are used against a house wall, it is effective to extend the planting beyond the corner of the building, possibly to the boundary line. This gives the house a longer appearance, and the horizontal line created is more pleasing than the sharp zigzag effect of typical foundation plantings.

Espaliers may form the basis for a special hobby garden where new material is tried or small plants are started that in a few years will be of sufficient size and interest to use in a prominent place, such as against the house near an entrance or in an outdoor living space. This kind of nursery garden may be started in an area formerly devoted to vegetables. Although it may be set off from the rest of the property, it needs good design. A grass panel through the center will lend an air of spaciousness and provide a simple foreground for prized espaliers.

ESPALIERS FOR CONTAINER GARDENING

The mobility of container-grown espaliers makes them useful for decorating a patio, or any other area where an interesting plant is wanted. While the plant is showy and in bloom, it can occupy an important place, then be moved to another part of the garden for the rest of the year. For the winter, container espaliers may be transferred out of tub or pot into a nursery bed for more protection, or tender specimens may be moved to a frost-free garage, cool basement, deep coldframe or pit, until danger of freezing passes.

Container-grown espaliers need rich, well-drained soil

kept evenly moist at all times and biweekly feedings of diluted liquid fertilizer throughout the active growing season. In addition, they need some means of support, as discussed in Chapter 2. See Section 3, Chapter 5, for a list of shrubs and trees suited to espaliering as container plants.

BASIC PATTERNS

There are numerous ways of training and using espaliered plants in the home garden. This chapter describes some basic espalier patterns, formal and informal. With these in mind, you will be able to select a site in your own garden and then choose a pattern and a plant suited to that location.

SOME FORMAL ESPALIER PATTERNS

The simplest espalier is a single cordon. This may be vertical, oblique or horizontal. The *single vertical cordon* (Figure 1) may be used at each end of fence-type espalier patterns such as the Belgian and arcure. In this position it gives the planting a finished appearance and helps to conceal the vertical post that supports the framework or trellis on which the espaliers are trained. Another use for the single vertical is to plant several on a chimney or other wall where strong vertical lines are desired. These give a formal effect if all are kept at the same height, informal if they are allowed to grow at random.

A single cordon planted at a 45-degree or oblique angle (Figure 1), either to right or left, is usually part of a fence- or screen-type espalier. If oblique cordons facing left and right are planted alternately in a row, the effect will be that of a Belgian fence.

The *single horizontal cordon* (Figure 1) consists of a vertical trunk with two horizontal branches extending in opposite directions. A *double horizontal cordon* (Figure 1) is a double-decked version of the single cordon. It is formed by allowing the center shoot to continue upward to about 18

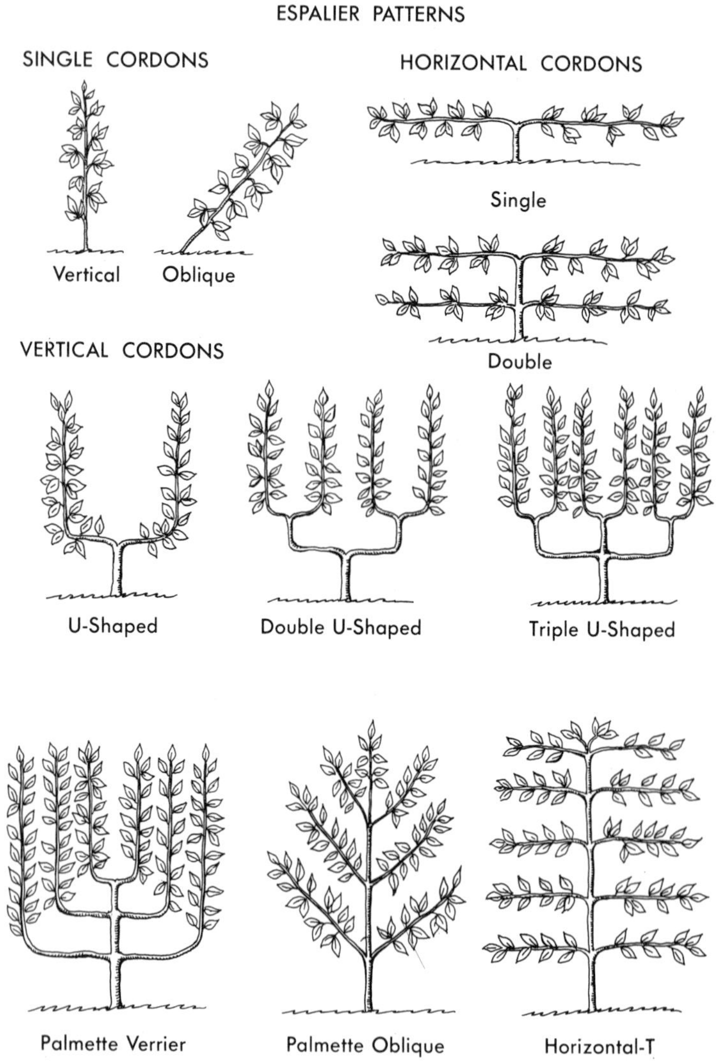

ESPALIER PATTERNS

SINGLE CORDONS   HORIZONTAL CORDONS

Vertical   Oblique

Single

Double

VERTICAL CORDONS

U-Shaped   Double U-Shaped   Triple U-Shaped

Palmette Verrier   Palmette Oblique   Horizontal-T

FIGURE   1

inches, where it is then pinched out to encourage the formation of two shoots, which are trained horizontally in opposite directions from each other and parallel to the two lower horizontal branches. This cordon makes an ideal screen between two parts of a garden, and it is excellent along a fence or in any narrow area, especially where the home gardener wants to grow fruit in a limited space.

The *vertical U-shape* (Figure 1) is a variation of the double cordon. This may be further embellished by making it double or even triple U-shaped (Figure 1). The *double vertical cordon* is a popular espalier pattern for planting on walls and for screening purposes.

The *palmette verrier* (Figure 1) is a favorite with landscape architects and homeowners. It is attained by training the branches of a horizontal cordon upward into a candelabra shape.

The *gridiron* (Figure 6) is still another variation of the single horizontal cordon. It is formed by training six branches parallel to each other and perpendicular to the cordon. While this pattern is especially useful for apples and pears, it is not difficult and adapts readily to any ornamental tree or shrub that has been trained as a single horizontal cordon.

The *palmette oblique* (Figure 1) may be low and broad or tall and narrow, depending on site and plant. Once this pattern is set, it can be trained without difficulty into a horizontal-T or palmette verrier.

The *horizontal-T* (Figure 1) is a multiple horizontal cordon that may be used against a wall or as a screen in the open if it is trained on a wire fence or other support. In addition, this is an excellent pattern for container-grown espaliers, as the supporting framework may consist simply of small pieces of redwood or aluminum tubing, with one vertical on which the horizontals are fastened at appropriate levels.

The *fan shape* (Figure 2) is most often seen as a free-form informal espalier with an over-all outline of a half-circle rising out of the ground. However, this may occasionally be so rigid as to become formal, with branches trained like the spokes of a wheel from a very low trunk or multistemmed out of the ground.

The *Belgian fence* (Figure 2) is another basic variation of the single horizontal cordon. By this method, branches are trained in opposite 45-degree angles, thus forming a broad V. When several of these are planted in a row, they form a lattice pattern. The *losange* (Figure 2) is a variation of the Belgian fence in which side branches are allowed to develop at spaced intervals to achieve considerable height and density within a relatively short period.

The *arcure* method (Figures 2 and 6) is another type of espalier fence. This is started by planting whips of suitable trees or shrubs about 3 feet apart in late winter or early spring. These are inserted at a slight angle, all leaning toward the right. After a few weeks the tip of each is curved over to form a half-circle and tied to the support. As shoots form along the whips, all are pinched back except the center one at the top of the curve. By August, it can be bent carefully in the opposite direction, where ultimately its tip will be tied into the base of the shoot formed on top of the curve to the left. This procedure is repeated as many years as necessary to achieve the completed arcure pattern of a desired height. It is interesting to note that after branches are bent downward, they cease to grow in length. This encourages abundant cropping in fruit trees, but the method is also an attractive way of training such ornamental shrubs as forsythia.

The imaginative gardener will think of many other ways in which to train espaliers in formal patterns. *Braiding* (Figure 2) is an example of the more unusual ways of espaliering. The gardener starts this form by planting two whips closely

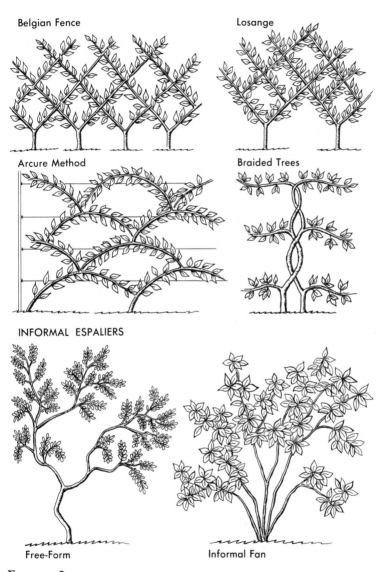

Belgian Fence

Losange

Arcure Method

Braided Trees

INFORMAL ESPALIERS

Free-Form

Informal Fan

FIGURE 2

together and allowing the bent trunks to form the first horizontal lines. Successive branches are braided upward, with side shoots encouraged to develop at appropriate levels to form other horizontals.

INFORMAL ESPALIER DESIGNS

The new concept for training plants into a flattened vertical plane is to allow them to grow in a casual or free-form design (Figures 2 and 3). In selecting a plant for this purpose, look for one that has an interesting trunk, branch and twig structure already. Sometimes a plant stunted by poor growing conditions or misshaped by accident will make a striking informal espalier.

Remember that while the informal espalier is among the most decorative and useful of all plants for today's gardens, it is not a formal espalier that has been allowed to go unpruned and out of bounds. True, the informal espalier does not usually require as much pruning and training as a formal pattern, but it is not something to be neglected season after season. Part of your success depends on thinning out certain twigs and leaving others, always striving to help the plant grow into an open and beautiful design.

The informal espalier is flattened into a vertical plane, but usually without the kind of supporting framework given to formal patterns. Occasionally a shrub or small tree can be pruned at planting time into a pleasing free-form espalier that needs no further training except the removal of future growth not in keeping with the design. However, most informal espaliers need some means of support, at least until they are established. You can train plants with tough stems by tying them to a piece of heavy-gauge copper wire or by using the special nails and rawl plugs described in Chapter 2.

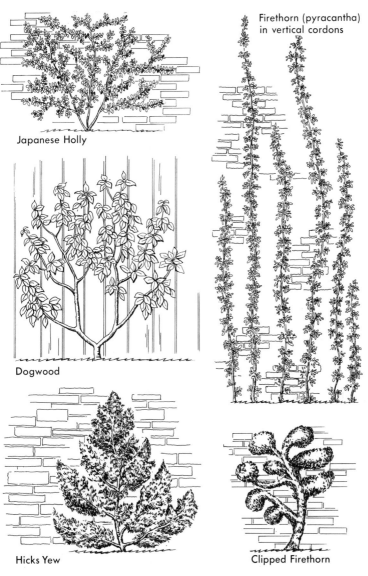

Japanese Holly

Firethorn (pyracantha)
in vertical cordons

Dogwood

Hicks Yew

Clipped Firethorn

Figure   3

2

Supports for Espaliers

All espaliers trained in formal patterns, and some of those in free-form designs, need a trellis or other framework as a means of supporting and training the branches. Usually this is put into place before the planting of shrub or tree, and its size is determined by the height and width the espalier may be expected to reach at maturity.

FREE-STANDING ESPALIER SUPPORTS

When an espalier planting serves to screen one area from another, the supporting framework will be free-standing. This may be as simple as utilizing an existing chain-link or similar wire fence, or it may require the erection of a special framework consisting of sturdy terminal posts with wires stretched taut between.

Suitable uprights for free-standing supports include 2- by 4-inch or 4- by 4-inch posts of weather-resistant wood such as cedar, redwood or cypress, or 1½-inch metal pipe. Set posts down 2 feet in the ground, preferably with the base of each in concrete. Space posts 8 to 10 feet apart, depending of course on the area to be covered, the espalier pattern to be used and the kind of plant to be supported. The first horizontal wire is generally placed 12 to 16 inches above the ground, with others spaced above this at regular intervals as needed. Use 10-gauge galvanized or copper wire or ³⁄₁₆-inch vinyl-coated tiller cable, with a 3-inch turnbuckle or straining bolt at one end so that it can be kept taut. In addition, if espalier patterns require right angles, it is important that all lines in the supporting framework be exactly horizontal or vertical.

After the basic support is in place, it is possible to add horizontal, vertical or diagonal arms to hold branches in place. Quarter- to half-inch bamboo poles fastened to the wire are excellent for this purpose. Wooden stakes (2 by 2 inches), driven 18 inches into the ground, make excellent vertical supports.

AIDS TO TRAINING ESPALIERS

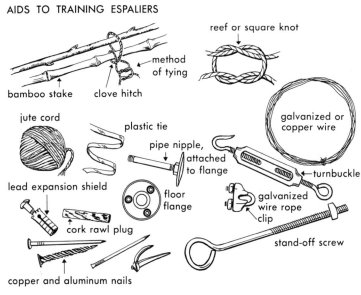

FIGURE 4

SUPPORTS FOR CONTAINER ESPALIERS

To support a container-grown espalier, use small strips of redwood, wire or bamboo. Anchor the framework by inserting the base several inches into the soil. It may also be necessary to attach frame to container with wire or small nails so that it will not move even slightly in wind.

Supports for container espaliers may follow the same patterns as those used for any espaliered plant. The horizontal-T (Figure 1) is probably the easiest to handle in a container as it requires only one vertical support, with horizontals wired or nailed at appropriate intervals.

SUPPORTS FOR ESPALIERS AGAINST WALLS

The first rule in locating an espalier by a solid wall is to place it at least 6 inches away to facilitate tying, pruning, circulation of air, spraying for pest control, and maintenance of building, such as painting. Any of the free-standing espalier supports may be placed next to a solid wall, but if the wall is of suitable material, fastening the support directly to it will usually result in a sturdy, inconspicuous frame for less expense and labor.

To attach a heavy-duty wire frame to a wall, use a 2¼-inch floor flange with a 6-inch galvanized nipple, threaded at both ends. For the wire, I recommend ³⁄₁₆-inch vinyl-coated tiller cable or 10-gauge copper wire. The cable may be obtained in any length or color (I prefer the clear plastic as it is least conspicuous) from companies that deal in motor boats and supplies. Buy the wire at a hardware store or building-supply house.

Make a loop with the cable or wire over the end of the galvanized nipple and fasten with a ³⁄₁₆-inch galvanized wire roof clip. At the opposite end, attach a 3-inch turn-buckle that has a hook at one end, to pull cable or wire taut. I find it best to place most horizontal wires 2 to 3 feet apart, and then to add short horizontal, vertical or diagonal arms as needed, using quarter- to half-inch bamboo poles fastened to the wire.

Attaching Supports to Masonry

For a masonry wall, lead expansion shields or rawl plugs may be placed in the mortared joints or in the brick or stone, and screw-eyes inserted. Make holes for these by using a star or carbide-tipped drill. See that the hole is barely large enough to hold the shields when they are tapped in with a hammer.

For less substantial wall supports, ample for all except large espaliers, use stand-off screws instead of the floor flanges and nipples. These can be obtained with shanks of sufficient length to keep the plant a few inches away from the wall. TV-antenna guides may also be used for this purpose. Sometimes copper or aluminum nails are simply driven into a wall, with copper wire strung from one to the other or the plant tied directly to the nails.

Wooden trellises make excellent supports for espaliers. One advantage is that when the wooden framework or trellis is located against a wall, it can be hinged at the bottom and hooked to the wall at the top to facilitate lowering the espalier at painting time or when the plant requires spraying for pest control. Strips of redwood, cypress or cedar are durable materials. The wooden espalier trellis may be built into any size or pattern. When carefully constructed, this kind of wooden support is an asset, serving to create the illusion of a completed espalier long before the plant itself reaches maturity.

SUPPORTING INFORMAL ESPALIERS

The informal espalier needs some means of support, at least at strategic intervals, in order to keep it flattened and also to allow the gardener to help the plant achieve a pleasing design of trunk and branches. One way to do this is to sink a long piece of heavy-gauge aluminum wire in the ground behind the espalier and to bend the wire into the desired design. Then train and tie the branches to follow it.

Another means of training the informal espalier is to use vine guides. These are special cement discs in which a short wire is embedded. They come in small packages, available at local garden centers and by mail from seed and garden-

IN MILD WINTER CLIMATES THE CHINESE HIBISCUS MAY BE ES-
PALIERED, AS HERE IN AN INFORMAL FAN SHAPE ON TRELLIS OF RED-
WOOD. WHERE WINTERS ARE COLD, PLANTS THAT WOULD GIVE A
SIMILAR EFFECT ARE CHINESE REDBUD, BURFORD HOLLY, AND DOUBLE-
FILE VIBURNUM.   (*William Aplin*)

supply firms. The discs are easily glued to wooden or masonry surfaces, but they are suitable only for small specimens, not for large tree-form espaliers. The pliable wire acts as a rest or support for the stem. It is not used as a tie, for if wire is pressed closely all around twig or branch, girdling results. Additional vine guides may be added as a plant grows; when a wall is painted, it is a simple matter to open the wires enough to release the stems.

An electrician's wall nail has a lead strap at the top that may also be used as a vine guide for training small formal and informal espaliers. This kind of nail is available at hardware stores; but do not confuse it with the large staple electricians use for holding wires in place, as this sort of nail is not suitable for training espaliers.

3

How to Plant and Start an Espalier

After you have studied the basic espalier patterns and designs, and have learned the ways to use them, your logical question will be how to obtain a proper plant. It is not difficult today to buy dwarf fruit trees already trained in various espalier patterns. However, only occasionally can ready-made espaliers of ornamental shrubs and trees be found. At present, gardeners on the West Coast will probably have more success than others in obtaining these, but with the increased interest in trained plants, it is more and more likely that young espalier specimens will become available at garden centers everywhere.

Do not be discouraged if you are unable to find nursery-trained espaliers. At the most, this means a delay of only a few years while a smaller plant of the selected ornamental shrub or tree is given a chance to develop under your own guidance. The alternative is to do some serious scouting for a misformed, one-sided plant that can, by some judicious pruning, be made to appear as an established espalier.

Well-developed specimen plants, then, are not the kind to seek when espaliering is desired. Instead, seek out a naturally flattened shrub with no major branches protruding, one that can be placed 6 to 12 inches from wall or trellis.

When you select this kind of plant, the nurseryman may try to better your selection by suggesting a perfectly symmetrical specimen, but be firm—you want height and width, not depth.

In selecting an espalier, keep uppermost in mind the mature size of the plant when it is trained by espaliering. You know the dimensions of the area to be planted. Select a plant which at maturity will be of a size appropriate to the site. Dwarf, low-, medium-, and tall-growing espaliers are listed by groups in Section 3 of Chapter 5.

Certain plants, particularly those of arching habit, can be trained to grow to two, three or even more times the height of a normal, mature specimen. Forsythia is a good example of this kind of plant. It may be trained as an espalier, perhaps as a vertical or horizontal cordon, to an almost indefinite height or length. On the other hand, certain other plants, particularly those of horizontal branching habit, can be restricted by pruning and careful training to much less than the normal mature height. Convexleaf holly, flowering quince and Dorothea crab apple are good examples. If pruning is done while branches are small, and a cut is made to a strong lateral branch, there will be no chopped- or headed-back appearance. Within a few months after pruning, the branches will look as if nature had intended them to grow that way.

PREPARE SOIL CAREFULLY

Any plant needs special care at transplanting time, and an espalier requires extra attention. A general rule is to dig out an area 3 feet square and about 2 feet deep, discard soil that is poor, and replace with a mixture of good garden loam combined with humus in the form of moist peatmoss or leafmold. It is wise to add some bonemeal or other mild organic fertilizer to the mixture but no strong nitrogenous fertilizer. Make the hole for the plant large enough so that roots can spread out freely.

Place a balled and burlapped plant carefully in the hole without breaking the soil ball. Unfasten the burlap at the top and roll the upper part to the side. Allow the burlap to remain on the side, and it will rot out in a year's time even before fine roots have grown through and beyond. Do not attempt to remove the burlap completely, as you may break the soil ball and expose roots to air.

If the new plant to be espaliered has been grown in a container, remove this with care. If a mat or net of roots is in evidence at the side, use a sharp knife to make several vertical slashes in the root system to encourage the formation of new vigorous roots.

After good soil has been firmed around the plants, water thoroughly, so that the moisture will seep down *to all the roots*. The first two years after transplanting are all-important to the success of a newly planted shrub or tree. In periods of dryness, when less than an inch of rain falls during any seven-day period, water new plants deeply so that the soil throughout the area remains nicely moist at all times.

TO START NEW ESPALIERS

The effects created by well-developed espaliers are always admired; it is no wonder that the enthusiastic gardener wants to find out how to grow his own either from young whips or by adapting larger specimens. Espaliering is not the easiest of training methods, but certainly it is not as difficult as developing a bonsai. Espaliering does require patience and some knowledge of pruning practices.

STARTING FORMAL ESPALIERS

The Horizontal Cordon

This espalier (Figure 1) is perhaps the easiest for the beginner. Purchase a young whip or "maiden" (a single stem without any major branching) and plant it 6 to 12 inches away from wall or trellis. Cut off the top at the height you want the first cordon to form (Figure 5). This will probably be 12 to 20 inches from the ground. Wait for new shoots. If you want only a single cordon to form, retain only the two best shoots, keeping in mind that they will be trained flat against wall or trellis, running parallel to the ground and in opposite directions from each other.

If a second cordon is wanted, retain the three best shoots, two to form the first cordon and the third to grow up as the central leader. When this attains a height of about 18 inches, usually by the beginning of the next year, cut it off at that point, and when new shoots form, select two for the second cordon. No others are retained unless a third cordon is desired. If so, the basic step is repeated with the third cordon, beginning the second spring after planting. Ultimately, if enough cordons are trained, this becomes the horizontal-T (Figure 1).

Vertical or U-Shaped Cordons

The single-U (Figure 1) is a simple variation of the single horizontal cordon. When the two horizontal branches reach a length of about 10 inches on either side, they are carefully bent to a vertical position and tied firmly to a lath or bamboo strip placed vertically. Usually about 16 inches is allowed between two vertical branches. The double- and triple-U forms are simply further developments of the single-U. To form either of these, the two verticals of the single-U are cut back to the height at which the new U's are wanted. The space between vertical branches in the U-forms is deter-mined largely by the individual plant and its size of leaf. Obviously, a small delicate leaf might be kept in closer ver-ticals than a large one of bold texture.

Palmette Verrier

Basically a variation of the horizontal cordon or horizontal-T with the branches trained into a candelabra form the palmette verrier (Figure 1) is sometimes called a gridiron, although I use the term for a slightly different pattern here (Figure 6). In my experience, shared by several other espalier growers, the central leader of the palmette verrier should not be allowed to remain after the pattern is complete. It is inclined to develop too rapidly and may ruin the design.

Horizontal-T

The training method for this pattern (Figure 1) is the same as for the horizontal cordon.

The Belgian Fence

This kind of espalier (Figure 2) is begun by planting whips upright against fence or frame, spacing them 18 to 24 inches apart, and using at least five to make an effective pattern. The whips are cut back to about 18 inches. When new shoots have begun to make growth, all but two are removed. These are trained at opposite 45-degree angles so that they make a diamond-shaped pattern against a wall or in the form of a screen to separate one part of the garden from another.

The Losange

An adaptation of the Belgian fence, the losange (Figure 2) is generally more adaptable to very small-leaved shrubs or to an area where considerable height is desired. By this method, two or more laterals are allowed to form from each of the two main branches. Spacing for these is determined by the individual plant, always with enough room left so that the design created by branches and leaves allows sufficient open space to set off the pattern effectively.

The Gridiron System

Basically this pattern (Figure 6) is another variation of the single horizontal cordon. Six vertical branches are allowed to rise parallel to each other from the single horizontal cordon,

THESE APPLE TREES ARE TRAINED IN THE BELGIAN FENCE PATTERN ON
REDWOOD SUPPORTS IN GARDENS OF THE UNITED NATIONS, NEW YORK.

(*Roche*)

three on either side of the main trunk. Later, if a more complicated design is desired, horizontals may be trained from each of the verticals. The result could be a striking geometrical design. Once a pattern has been set, it is retained by pruning branches to the desired level each winter, or after flowering time in late spring or early summer.

The Arcure System

This type of espalier fence or screen (Figures 2 and 6) starts with whips 3 to 4 feet tall, planted at a slight angle to the right. Sometime within the first few months after planting, but after roots have settled down and growth has begun, bend each whip over to form a semicircle or half-moon and tie the tip to the wire frame or other support.

Several laterals will then occur on the upper side of the curved stem, and possibly some on the lower part. As soon as possible, remove all of these except the center one on top. This one is encouraged to grow unhampered. By the following August or September, it can be bent in the opposite direction to form another arching shape or half-circle. There it is tied to the support approximately 18 inches above the point at which the first branch was tied down.

This arching process may be continued, first one way and then the other, for as many years as necessary to reach the height desired. No laterals are allowed to form except those in the center of an arched branch when these are wanted to form new arches. It is interesting to note that very little pruning is needed on the older arches, as they increase almost not at all in length after being curved down.

The arcure system is useful with many ornamental shrubs such as forsythia, and ideal for dwarf fruit trees, as it induces the development of fruit buds early in the life of a tree. Fruit bearing thus begins much sooner than on standard trees. In addition, trees grown in this pattern are wind-resistant.

STARTING INFORMAL ESPALIERS

It is difficult to give specific directions for creating a shape that is determined almost entirely by the individual plant. However, even in working with informal designs for espaliers, there are certain similarities. One of these is the *fan*

ESPALIERS MAY BE ADAPTED TO ALL TYPES OF ARCHITECTURE. HERE THEY ARE USED WITH FRENCH PROVINCIAL. THE PLANTS ARE PLUM TREES (LEFT AND RIGHT) WITH A LOQUAT IN THE CENTER. IN COLD CLIMATES, A MAGNOLIA MIGHT BE USED IN PLACE OF THE LOQUAT.
(Max Tatch)

shape, frequently achieved with any tree or shrub that tends to be multiple-stemmed from a very low trunk, or perhaps multiple-stemmed out of the ground. While the fan shape may occasionally be so rigid as to be formal, it is most often seen as a free and easy informal espalier with an over-all outline of a half-circle rising out of the ground. The fan shape can be used to create a beautiful effect against house or garden wall. The cotoneaster is especially well-suited to its use.

The *fountain shape* is similar to the fan except that several stems rise vertically, originating from about the same point on the trunk, and spread gradually until they begin to cascade into a flattened fountain shape.

The third basic shape often seen in an informal espalier is a modified *Hogarth curve*. This is particularly effective with contemporary architecture where there are large expanses of unadorned wall.

The informal espalier is more likely to be developed from a mature plant than are the formal patterns that need careful training from the time they are young. If you are working with a plant of considerable size and age, you can usually establish the general framework for an informal espalier in the first pruning. Cut off branches that stick out from the wall. Also, remove those that cross each other, as well as any that develop as verticals near the top where they would be contrary to the more or less established design of the espalier. Usually these branches need to be removed by making a flush cut at the main stem, although occasionally it may be better to cut back to a bud on a lateral branch.

The objective with informal espaliers is to develop a flattened plant that is beautiful in a free-form design, open enough to allow the texture and color of the wall to show. To maintain this effect, additional thinning out of twigs and branches will be necessary from time to time.

4

Good Training and Good Health

The training of espaliers is accomplished largely through frequent pruning and tying. These steps are necessary whether you start with a young unbranched whip, an established shrub or tree or an espalier trained in a pattern.

TOOLS FOR PRUNING

You will need a sharp pruning knife and a pair of hand shears or pruners. The pruning of espalier plants requires a light touch—that is, attention to each branch. Heavy-handed pruning with long-bladed clippers destroys a plant's natural beauty, whereas in a well-trained espalier, the fine qualities of leaf, stem, flower and fruit are emphasized. Use small pruning shears, and think twice before you cut once.

SOME GENERAL PRUNING RULES FOR ESPALIERS

Do heavy pruning to shape an espalier while a plant is dormant, preferably before new foliage has developed in spring. On established plants where flowers are a consideration, do this pruning immediately after flowering, but before July.

On all except very slow-growing plants, light pruning of new growth may be done every three to four weeks during the

29

active growing season. This will consist of a light snipping with hand shears or pinching with fingers to maintain the desired pattern. If a pruning or two is missed during the summer, no serious harm will be done, since a slightly heavier pruning can be given later.

Do not attempt heavy pruning in July, August or September as this would encourage the production of abundant new growth that would not have time to mature or harden before cold weather. Such growth would be subject to dieback or winterkill.

In pruning espaliers, as with other trees or shrubs, do not leave short stubs devoid of foliage or buds. Such stubs are not only unsightly, they cannot heal over to prevent the ingress of fungi that cause rotting of the main stem. This problem can be serious with larger branches of trees. Rarely are the pruning cuts of shrubs painted, but when cuts on deciduous trees are more than ½-inch in diameter they need to be covered with special tree paint. This can be purchased at local garden centers or by mail from seed and garden-supply firms. Needle evergreens are rich in resins, and thereby provide their own protective covering. It is best to remove branches when they are small so that no large scars result and healing is quickly effected.

Pruning determines the direction of future growth. A new limb will sprout in the direction the top bud is facing. Therefore, have end buds face in the direction of desired new growth (Figure 5).

Root pruning is not ordinarily practiced on espaliers, but it can be useful if a plant is inclined to grow larger than is desirable for its location. This is done in early spring with a long, thin-bladed spade. Insert the blade to full depth in the ground 3 to 4 feet from the main trunk (the distance may be more or less, depending on the size of the specimen), and repeat until the plant has been completely encircled. This

BASIC PRUNING STEPS FOR ESPALIERS

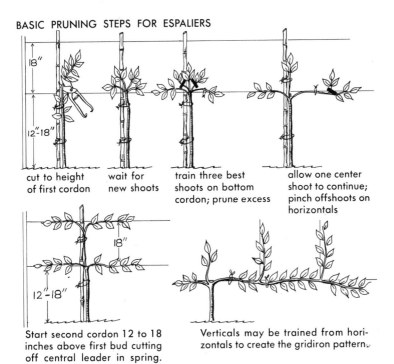

| cut to height of first cordon | wait for new shoots | train three best shoots on bottom cordon; prune excess | allow one center shoot to continue; pinch offshoots on horizontals |

Start second cordon 12 to 18 inches above first bud cutting off central leader in spring.

Verticals may be trained from horizontals to create the gridiron pattern.

PRUNING TIPS

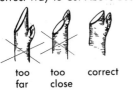

branch to cut · cut close · never leave stub

Correct Way to Cut Above Bud

too far   too close   correct

Pruning determines direction of future growth. A new limb will sprout in the direction the top bud is facing. Have end buds face in direction of desired new growth.

FIGURE 5

pruning severs wide-spreading feeder roots, and curtails rampant growth.

ESPALIERS NEED A GUIDING HAND

Whether a tree or shrub used as an espalier is placed in a formal or informal design, it needs a firm guiding hand to direct placement of branches. A trellis or other type of support is the basic guide for training, but it cannot be effective without tying. Small, tender branches may be held in place with raffia or rubber budding strips. For heavier branches, use soft cotton twine, jute garden cord or raffia. It is important that the finished tie allow some room for the branch to expand. Loop the tie around the support first, then around the branch. Use a reed or square knot on the support to finish the tying process (Figure 4).

Plastic- or paper-covered wire is not recommended as tying material for woody plants unless it can be checked and renewed frequently. Remember, a wire may be loose when applied, but after a year or two, it may be tight enough to cut off the portion of the plant above it. For this reason, always remove immediately any wired labels that come on plants.

Tying is a part of espalier training that must be done constantly through the growing season as required. It is important to do this frequently, before branches get too far out of line. No matter how pliable a branch may be, if you want to change its shape drastically you may have to achieve this gradually, until finally the desired shape is achieved (Figure 6). To make the complete change in one step may result in needless damage.

GOOD HEALTH MEASURES

In addition to regular pruning and tying, feeding is an important aspect of espalier culture. Too much fertilizer with a high nitrogen content is to be avoided, for it may make a tree or shrub nearly impossible to maintain in the pattern desired. However, some feeding is needed to maintain healthy foliage, to encourage flowers, and to stimulate fruit production if the plant is grown for fruit.

Fertilizers for the home garden are usually sold in "complete" mixtures; that is, they contain the basic elements essential to plant growth—nitrogen, phosphorus, and potassium (abbreviated N–P–K). The percentages of these that a mixture contains are given on the package, for example, 10–6–4, meaning that the product contains 10 per cent nitrogen, 6 per cent phosphorus and 4 per cent potassium. Inert materials, necessary in manufacturing or packaging the fertilizer, make up the balance, 80 per cent in this case.

Probably you have also heard about chemical and organic fertilizers. The organics include steamed bonemeal, cottonseed meal, bloodmeal, and manure. The N–P–K ratio for

BY THE SECOND OR THIRD YEAR AFTER PLANTING, ESPALIERED FRUIT TREES LIKE THIS APPLE, BLOSSOM FREELY AND BEGIN CROPPING.

(*McFarland*)

dried manure varies but is usually about 1–1–1. Cottonseed meal is excellent as a fertilizer for plants that require an acid soil. Dried blood rates high in nitrogen, but as a rule is seldom used in the culture of espaliers. Bonemeal is likely to have a N–P–K ratio of 1–15–0, although it does not always have this much phosphorus (the middle figure). Since it is a mild fertilizer that does not cause burning or excessive vegetative growth, it may be used around newly transplanted stock or for container-grown specimens.

Chemical fertilizers give satisfactory results when they are used according to container directions. An excessive amount may burn the feeder roots of plants or induce rapid growth, which is not the aim in developing a good espalier. If applied without any regularity, chemical fertilizers tend to make a plant grow in spurts, a trait definitely not desirable for espaliers. If you are undecided about the brand of fertilizer to use, ask your county agricultural agent, or send to the agricultural extension service or the agricultural experiment station at your state university for bulletins on the subject. They have prepared material for your specific area.

As a rule espaliers will benefit from light feedings of a 5–10–5 fertilizer in spring and through the summer until July. Fertilizing done toward late summer and into fall encourages new growth that does not have sufficient time to harden before cold weather sets in. This will probably be killed back.

Work the fertilizer into the ground around the plant, and then water the area well. If there is sod around the plant, make holes with a metal bar so you can apply the fertilizer below the grass roots.

You may also see at local garden centers certain fertilizers labeled *Azalea-Camellia Food* or *Rhododendron Food*. Generally these contain a nitrogen carrier selected to give an acid reaction.

PROTECTION FROM HARMFUL ELEMENTS

Insects. An espalier is subject to the same insects that might attack the plant if it were growing naturally. A plant used against a south or west wall and exposed to full sun is especially prone to infestations of scale and aphids.

Diseases. Plants espaliered directly on a wall where air circulation may not be free around the branches are subject to foliage diseases such as blackspot and powdery mildew.

Pest Control Measures

When spraying espaliers trained on walls, use materials that will not stain. Generally, for insect control, sevin, malathion, DDT, or lindane will not leave discoloring residue. Captan is an effective spray for diseases. Nicotine sulfate is likely to discolor wood, particularly if it is used with a spreader-sticker such as soap.

If an espalier becomes infested with scale, the best thing to do is to carefully paint an oil emulsion spray on trunk and branches, thus taking care of the scale infestation but keeping the background wall free of discoloration. However, scale insects are most easily controlled when they are in the crawling stage, and this varies with different types of scale. Identification can be determined with the help of your county agricultural agent. Malathion and sevin are effective sprays on scale insects that are in the crawling stage.

Other Protective Measures for Espaliers

Plants of borderline hardiness trained as espaliers against south and west walls are subject to sunscald. This may occur in the summer, but is more likely to happen in the winter. Sunscald and wind damage can be mitigated by spraying with raw anti-desiccant like Wilt-Pruf. Damage can also be prevented to some extent by wrapping trunks with coarse fabric or a special paper called Tree-Wrap manufactured for this purpose (available at local garden centers and by mail from seed and garden-supply firms). Strong winds may cause damage in any case unless espaliers are securely tied to sturdy supports.

When an espalier receives attentive pruning and tying, is fed well early in the season and given evenly moist soil and protection from insect or disease attack, it will be much less likely to present other cultural problems.

5

Fifty Fine Ornamentals
to Espalier—Acer to Viburnum

This chapter is divided into three sections: the first explains the terms used; the second describes ornamental plants suited to espaliering; and the third is a guide to landscape uses of espaliers. It will pay you to study Section 1 to know exactly what each of the descriptive phrases in Section 2 means. The lists in Section 3 will serve as handy guides in selecting espalier plants for your climate, and for any special sites.

SECTION 1—BY WAY OF EXPLANATION

Nomenclature

We all take pleasure in knowing our friends by first names, but if the telephone directory were arranged on a John-Mary-Bill basis, it would be most confusing. So it is with plants. If we don't have the complete botanical name, problems arise. The more we extend ourselves beyond the simple listing of one variety each, for example, of barberry, lilac, and privet, the more we recognize the necessity of knowing complete plant names. This is not meant to discourage the use of any common names—certainly they are important, and we need to know them also.

As with people, there are not enough different common names to go around. Further, an individual may be known by one nickname in one place and by another elsewhere. "Ironwood" is a good common name, but it is applied to more than one plant, and the same is true of locust and gum. The white water-lily of Europe has over a hundred common names, but botanists agree on one simple scientific name—*Nymphaea alba*—that is the same the world over.

For the descriptions given in Section 2, the plants have been arranged alphabetically according to botanical names. In addition, the family and common names are included. All common names are cross-referenced in the Index to help you find any plant whose botanical name you do not know.

Pronunciation

See "How to Pronounce Plant Names," Appendix B.

Hardiness

A plant that grows successfully in one section of the country may languish or fail in another. A common reason for this is varietal difference in reaction to low temperatures. However, other factors may account for a plant's inability to survive. The soil may be too alkaline or too acid, or it may be poorly drained or excessively dry. Strong, drying winds or high summer temperatures may be the deciding factor. With regard to broadleaf evergreens, a southern exposure with full winter sun combined with frozen ground may be double-acting in its deleterious effects. Plants are activated by the sun when they need to be semidormant and therefore the leaves require extra moisture that frozen roots are unable to provide.

Do not judge a given variety on the basis of one trial. A plant may have failed to survive the winter because it has been poorly planted or has been unfavorably located on your property. A plant of borderline hardiness will fail if placed in a frost pocket or other low-lying moist land that encourages late growth not able to mature before severe freezing weather occurs. An abnormally dry fall followed by an early freeze cuts off the water supply that is needed even in winter. Young plants that have not had time to develop deep root systems are more sensitive to freezing temperatures than are larger, well-established specimens. Shallow-rooted trees and shrubs, including those newly planted, benefit from a deep mulch applied after ground is frozen. Mulching prevents deep freezing yet keeps ground frozen at the surface. This forestalls alternate thawing and freezing, a harmful action that may expose roots to wind and sun.

Many things can happen to a plant during the winter, and frequently it is difficult to pinpoint the exact condition that kills or weakens. Nevertheless, the extent of a plant's ability to survive the severity of winter cold is a factor that determines whether or not it will live in a specific area. Maps have been prepared based on minimum winter temperatures, and plants have been keyed to these maps to indicate northern limits of the area in which they may be expected to grow. These maps have certain limitations, in that small but significant changes of elevation within a relatively small area cannot be indicated. Even on a half-acre of land there can be noticeable variation. Such deviations within a small area are referred to as microclimates. Regardless of such limitations, maps that show zones of hardiness are excellent guides in selecting plants most likely to prove suitable in a particular area.

The map used as an endpaper in this book is a duplicate of a portion of one prepared in 1960 by the United States Department of Agriculture and the National Arboretum cooperating with the American Horticultural Society. This map portrays a more detailed division of area than was shown in the 1948 USDA map. The older map has been widely used, but zones 4, 5 and 6 are markedly different on the two maps. The plants listed in this book are keyed to the 1960 map.

On the large colored copies of the 1960 map (Miscellaneous Publication #814, *Plant Hardiness Zone Map*, available for 15 cents from the Superintendent of Documents, United States Government Printing Office, Washington 25, D.C.), each zone is further divided into *a* and *b* sectors representing a 5-degree change in temperature in contrast to the 10-degree changes between zones. For simplicity, the subdivisions indicating *a* and *b* sectors have not been included in the reduced map of this book. However, in the descriptions, Section 2, some plants carry one of these numerals after the zone number. This indicates that the *a* plants are somewhat hardier than other plants carrying the same zone number and thus can be more safely grown in northern parts of the designated zone. Those labeled *b* are more adaptable to southern parts of the zone. The approximate range of average annual minimum temperatures for each zone is:

Zone 3: −40 to −30 degrees
Zone 4: −30 to −20 degrees
Zone 5: −20 to −10 degrees
Zone 6: −10 to   0 degrees
Zone 7:   0 to 10 degrees

Sun and Shade

In giving the culture for a plant described in Section 2, *sun* indicates a position that receives full sun during most of the day. *Partial shade* means full sun for a few hours of the day or dappled shade such as that provided by high-headed trees throughout most of the day. *Full shade* describes a position that receives open light but little if any direct sun.

Mature Height

In the descriptions of Section 2 the expected height as an espalier has been given. This may be considerably higher or lower than standard size because of the variation made possible by espaliering.

Evergreen, Deciduous

Evergreen indicates a plant that retains foliage year after year, even through periods of cold weather. A *deciduous* plant may be termed *leaf-losing;* that is, the foliage drops off in autumn or early winter and does not reappear until suitably warm weather the following spring. Occasionally a plant may be listed as *semievergreen.* This indicates that toward the plant's northern limits branches and twigs, but not foliage, may survive cold temperatures.

Flowering Time

This varies from year to year, especially with the first trees and shrubs that bloom after winter. From year to year there can be as much as a month's difference in the date of earliest bloom. As the season progresses, this time spread is narrowed. Spring begins in the South, and along the eastern seaboard its moves northward at the rate of 10 to 15 miles per day. The flowering dates used in this book are from the records of Dr. Donald Wyman of the Arnold Arboretum near Boston. Plants that flower in the Boston area during mid-May will bloom in New York City in early May. The opening day will advance toward the South so that in northern Florida it would be mid-March.

SECTION 2—ORNAMENTAL PLANTS FOR ESPALIERING

The use of ornamental plants as espaliers is in its infancy. Plants that have not yet been widely tried may prove to be exciting subjects. The plants described are not intended as the last word. Other plants are worth trying, and it is certain that some may prove to be equal to if not better than some listed here.

How do we judge whether a plant is appropriate for espaliering? First, it needs as many good characteristics as possible. Structural form and branching habit, texture, foliage, winter color of twigs and older bark, ornamental fruit, flowers, resistance to insects and disease, and hardiness are all taken into consideration. In addition, especially for training espaliers into informal patterns, supple branches are necessary.

The rate at which a plant grows is all-important in considering it for an espalier. The amount of pruning necessary depends on whether the right plant is chosen for a site. The space to be covered may be 3 by 3 feet or 30 by 30 feet. It is improbable that the same plant would be ideal in both situations. There are dwarfs and giants among espaliers, making it possible to have a wide choice for any location.

| ACER | *Aceraceae* | Bloodleaf Japanese Maple |
| | | Spiderleaf Japanese Maple |

A. palmatum atropurpureum, bloodleaf or red Japanese maple, from Korea and Japan, is a deciduous small tree, round-topped, with an irregular crown and low side branches that give a multiple-stemmed effect. Height as an espalier— 10 to 30 feet. Leaf—2 to 3½ inches long and as wide, deeply divided into five to seven lobes. Red foliage all season, brighter in autumn, but not as brilliant as the green-leaved types when those turn. Several varieties, such as Bloodgood, have been selected for darker summer color.

CULTURE: Zone 6a. Sun to partial shade; if site is too shady, red changes to green by midsummer. Soil—rich, well-drained and cool. Transplant with a ball of soil around roots, preferably in spring. Provide ample moisture in dry season.

USES: Formal or informal, especially where height is needed. May be used as a tubbed plant if minimum size is maintained. Pattern of sharply cut leaves, enhanced by the removal of some branches, provides a striking silhouette. The type plant, *A. palmatum*, with plain green leaves, is preferable where the color of a red form is not pleasing.

A. palmatum ornatum, spiderleaf Japanese maple, a deciduous small tree of garden origin, is round-topped with an irregular crown and pendulous branches that cascade sometimes to the ground. Height as an espalier—3 to 8 feet. Leaf —deeply and finely divided, the seven finger-like sections joined to a central stalk. Dark red all season. The rare *A. p. dissectum* (sometimes listed as *A. p. multifidum* and *A. p. palmatifidum*) is similar except that it has green foliage.

CULTURE: Zone 6a. See *Acer palmatum atropurpureum*.

USES: Informal, on fence, one-story wall, or as a tubbed specimen.

ARCTOSTAPHYLOS   *Ericaceae*   Bearberry

A. uva-ursi, native to eastern North America, is a prostrate broadleaf evergreen. Height as an espalier—6 to 15 feet. Leaf—1 inch long, a third as wide, green turning bronze in winter. Flower—pink or white, in spring, followed by red berries. Sometimes called kinnikinnick.

CULTURE: Zone 3 (may be hardy in Zone 2b). Sun to partial shade. Soil—light, acid and evenly moist. Difficult to transplant except when purchased container-grown from a nurseryman. Plant in early spring or fall in a soil mixture of equal parts well-rotted acid leafmold (German or Canadian peatmoss may be used instead) and clean sharp sand.

USES: Informal. This trailing shrub needs careful and frequent tying to the support, but when established it makes a distinctive espalier.

CAMELLIA   *Theaceae*   Japanese Camellia

C. japonica, from China and Japan, is a broadleaf evergreen shrub of oval form, becoming treelike in the deep South.

Height as an espalier—10 to 30 feet. Leaf—dark, glossy and leathery, to 4 inches long. Flowers—single, semidouble or double, in many colors and combinations, from white to pink to dark red, appearing in winter and early spring. Varieties that do well as espaliers include Bride's Bouquet, Elegans,

BEARBERRY (*Arctostaphylos uva-ursi*) SHOWS ITS ATTRACTIVE RED BARK AGAINST THE WHITE BRICK OF HOUSE. THIS TRAILING PLANT IS TRAINED UPRIGHT BY MEANS OF METAL HOOKS FASTENED TO BRICK.

(*Jeannette Grossman*)

English Magnoliaeflora, French Imperator, Lady Clare, Masterpiece, Southern Donckelari and Ville de Nantes.

CULTURE: Zone 7. Partial shade. Protect from winter sun and strong winds. Soil—light, acid and evenly moist. After flowering and again in late autumn feed with an azalea-camellia fertilizer or with cottonseed meal. For a plant 2 to 3 feet tall, use one-half pound of fertilizer; a plant 8 to 10 feet tall will need three to four pounds.

USES: Formal or informal on fence, wall, or in a tub. Conspicuous blossoms and excellent evergreen foliage make camellias favorite espalier plants in warmer climates. Northern limits are gradually being extended by varieties selected for cold tolerance, especially if planted in a protective place. The sasanqua camellias with a hardiness rating of Zone 7b, are sometimes preferred for their smaller leaves, daintier flowers and greater sun tolerance than the Japonicas. Good sasanquas for espaliering include Dawn, Hiryo (Red Bird), Hugh Evans (Hebe), Mine-No-Yuki (White Doves) and Showa-No-Sakae.

CARAGANA   *Leguminosae*   Lorberg Siberian Pea-Tree

C. arborescens lorbergi, a deciduous shrub of broad columnar, irregular form and pendulous branches, from Siberia. Height as an espalier—6 to 30 feet. Leaf—3 inches long and compound. The light green foliage gives a delicate, lacy effect. The branches are green. Flowers—pale yellow, pealike, with many in a cluster in mid-May. Sometimes called ferny caragana.

CULTURE: Zone 3. Sun or partial shade. Soil—light to rich. This plant grows rapidly, is tolerant of a variety of soils, and is seldom bothered by pests.

USES: Informal, wherever a plant of fine texture is wanted. Graceful branching, delicate flowers, and green stems for winter interest make this notable.

CEDRUS   *Pinaceae*   Blue Atlas Cedar

C. atlantica glauca, from North Africa, is a needle evergreen tree that forms a broad, pyramidal shape with lower
branches horizontal and spreading. At maturity, it tends to
be flat-topped. Height as an espalier—10 to 30 feet. The
short, pale blue-green needles grow as a whorl on short spurs.
The 3-inch cones are borne upright.

CULTURE: Zone 7a. Sun. Soil—rich and well-drained.
Transplant with a ball of soil in spring.

USES: Formal or informal. This tree's soft coloring makes
it very attractive. Each cluster of needles looks like a minia-
ture tree, and gives a sculptured effect to an individual stem
silhouetted against a wall. If grown as a lawn specimen, the
tree would take up considerable space. When it is given the
protection of a wall, it can be grown farther north. This is a
true cedar in contrast to the common red-cedar, which is
really a juniper.

CERCIS   *Leguminosae*   White Redbud
                                                        Chinese Redbud

C. canadensis alba, the white redbud found in southwestern
Missouri prior to 1901, is a deciduous small tree with an
irregularly rounded top. Where low side branches are maintained, the effect of a multiple-stemmed tree is gained. Height
as an espalier—10 to 30 feet. Leaf—light green, rounded, 3
to 5 inches long, and about as wide. Stems—dark in color
and angular in growth habit. Flowers—pure white in mid-
May, appearing not only on the younger wood but on large
stems and even on the trunk. The Eastern redbud (*C.
canadensis*), native from New Jersey to Missouri and south-
west, is common in some areas, has a magenta flower that is
not always admired. In recent years, better color selections,
such as Wither's Pink Charm and Pinkbud, have been made.

CULTURE: Zone 5b. Soil—rich, humus-like, and well-drained. Provide ample moisture during periods of drought. Avoid heavy, sticky soils. Redbuds have a spreading root system that makes them difficult to transplant except while small, or after frequent root pruning. Transplant in spring.

USES: Informal.

C. chinensis, the Chinese redbud, introduced before 1850 from Central China, is a deciduous shrub with an irregularly rounded top, and several stems arising from the base. Height as an espalier—3 to 8 feet. Leaf—round with heart-shaped base, at least 3 inches long and equally wide. Dark-colored twigs. Flowers—pealike, larger, deeper colored, and more numerous than those of the Eastern redbud, in mid-May. Sometimes called Chinese Judas-tree.

CULTURE: Zone 6b. See *Cercis canadensis alba.*

USES: Informal. Bright flowers and angular twigs make this redbud valuable as an espalier.

CHAENOMELES	*Rosaceae*	Flowering Quince Chinese Quince

C. lagenaria, the flowering quince, introduced from China before 1800, is a deciduous shrub, irregularly round-topped, with spreading, semihorizontal, angular branches. Height as an espalier—3 to 15 feet. The foliage is dark green, glossy and leathery, 3 inches long and 1½ inches wide, with two rounded leaflike stipules at the base. Flowers—various shades of red to pale pink or white, in early May, followed by large yellow fruit useful for making jelly. The numerous named varieties offer a good color selection. Porcelain Rose holds its foliage late in the season. Sometimes listed as *Cydonia japonica.*

CULTURE: Zone 5. Soil—heavy; in well-drained, sandy soil the quince will drop its foliage soon after midsummer. The best flowers are produced in a sunny location, although the plant will thrive in shade. Grows rapidly, transplants

easily and has few pests, although scale may be troublesome.
Uses: Informal.

C. sinensis, the Chinese quince introduced from China about
1800, is a deciduous shrub that may become treelike. Height
as an espalier—10 to 30 feet. Leaf—rounded, 2 to 3 inches
long, dark green, leathery, turning scarlet in autumn.
Flowers—pale pink in May. The trunk has attractive, flak-
ing bark.

Culture: Zone 6. Soil—light or heavy. Sun or shade.
Tolerant of a variety of conditions. May not flower in its
northern limits, but the foliage and bark remain as assets.

Uses: Informal.

CORNUS	*Cornaceae*	Japanese Dogwood
		Cornelian Cherry

C. kousa, the Japanese dogwood, from Japan and Korea, was
introduced in 1875. It is a deciduous, small tree that lends
itself to training as a multiple-stemmed plant. The upper
branches are vertical but others spread out horizontally.
Height as an espalier—10 to 30 feet. Leaf—3 inches long,
little more than 1 inch wide. Fall color is russet-red, and
comes late so that the plant is best located on high ground
not subject to early frosts. The so-called flowers are actually
bracts, as is true of the more generally known flowering dogwood (*Cornus florida*). Bracts do not have the fragility of
petals and remain showy for three or four weeks. They are
white, long-pointed, and produced in abundance throughout
the month of June. Fruit—pale red, resembling a small
strawberry. The bark flakes off in the manner of a sycamore
so that older specimens have special winter interest. The
Chinese dogwood (*C. chinensis*), introduced from China in
1907, has a wider bract than the type and thus it is even
more showy.

CULTURE: Zone 5b. Sun or shade. Soil—rich, but sandy-textured and well-drained. An azalea-camellia fertilizer mixed with leafmold makes a good stimulant if this plant is slow in getting started.

USES: Formal or informal.

DOGWOOD TRAINED AS AN INFORMAL ESPALIER MAKES A DELIGHTFUL FOCAL POINT FOR AN OUTDOOR LIVING AREA.   (*Paul E. Genereux*)

C. mas, the Cornelian cherry, from central and southern Europe and western Asia, has been cultivated since ancient times, and was used in Colonial gardens. It is a deciduous shrub, round-headed and dense. Older specimens may attain the stature of a small tree with lower branches that sweep the ground. Height as an espalier—10 to 30 feet. Leaf—rounded, 2 inches long by 1½ wide, dark green with little or no fall color, although held until late on the tree. Flower—small, pale yellow in April followed by bright red fruit resembling a large elongated cherry and ripening in late summer; sour but edible. The Japanese Cornelian cherry (*C. officinalis*) has larger flowers, earlier in the season.

CULTURE: Zone 5. Soil—rich and well-drained. Partial shade to full sun. Easily transplanted and seldom troubled by pests.

USES: Formal or informal.

CORYLUS   *Betulaceae*   Purpleleaf Filbert

C. maxima purpurea, from southeastern Europe and western Asia, is a deciduous shrub of irregularly rounded form with many upright slender branches. Height as an espalier—6 to 25 feet. Leaf—2 to 4 inches long, 2 to 3 inches wide, dark purple all season. Light colored catkins, 2 to 2½ inches long, in early April. The branches are flexible. Formerly listed as *C. m. atropurpurea* and *C. avellana purpurea.* May be called purpleleaf hazelnut. *C. avellana contorta,* Harry Lauder's walking stick, has twisted and curled branches that are of particular interest during the winter and early spring.

CULTURE: Zone 5. Full sun is needed to retain colorful foliage. Soil—light or heavy, but moist in summer. Grows rapidly.

USES: Formal or informal. The dark purple leaf is attractive against a light-colored surface; nearby plants need to be of a neutral color so as not to present a conflict of interest.

Branches pruned in full foliage are useful for flower arrangements indoors.

COTONEASTER   *Rosaceae*   Spreading Cotoneaster
                                           Franchet Cotoneaster
                                           Rock Cotoneaster
                                           Hardy Willowleaf Cotoneaster

C. divaricata, the spreading cotoneaster, introduced in 1907 from central and western China, is a deciduous shrub of arching branches and numerous fine twigs. Height as an espalier—3 to 15 feet. Leaf—¾-inch long, about ½-inch wide, dark green and glossy, turning to dark red in autumn. Flowers—not conspicuous, but followed by red berries in the fall.

CULTURE: Zone 5b. Sun. Soil—rich or light, but always well-drained. Transplant with a ball of soil in the spring. Lace bug may be troublesome.

USES: Informal. Most cotoneasters naturally form branches in flat sprays that espalier well.

C. francheti, the Franchet cotoneaster, introduced in 1895 from western China, is a deciduous shrub of widely arching branches. Height as an espalier—3 to 15 feet. Leaf—1 inch long, half as wide, gray-green with a lighter color on the tomentose undersurface, orange-red in autumn. Young twigs are covered with fine hairs. Flowers—not significant, but orange-red berries are colorful in autumn.

CULTURE: Zone 6. See *Cotoneaster divaricata.*

USES: Informal. The gray-green summer foliage, supple twigs and autumn berries make this an excellent espalier plant.

C. horizontalis, the rock cotoneaster, introduced in 1880 from western China, is a deciduous to semievergreen shrub, flat-topped and wide-spreading. Height as an espalier—1 to

4 feet. Leaf—rounded, ½-inch or less in length, and dark glossy green changing to orange-red in autumn. Fruit—abundant, bright red, long-lasting. Stems—supple and will mold themselves over a rock or ledge. Sometimes called rock spray.

CULTURE: Zone 6. See *Cotoneaster divaricata.*

USES: Informal. A small, refined plant for a low wall; when used in this way it has the appearance of a closely clinging vine. A principal stem with its side branches arranged in a fishbone pattern makes a delightful espalier.

C. salicifolia floccosa, the hardy willowleaf cotoneaster, introduced in 1908 by Ernest "Chinese" Wilson, from western China, is a broadleaf evergreen shrub of arching branches. Height as an espalier—6 to 30 feet. Leaf—2 to 3 inches long, narrow, somewhat rugose, dark green and semiglossy, bronzy red during colder months. Red fruits persist into winter.

CULTURE: Zone 6b. Partial shade or sun. Soil—rich and well-drained. Transplant with a ball of soil in late spring. Fireblight may be troublesome in some areas. If so, cut out the diseased portion; sterilize cutting tools in alcohol.

USES: Formal or informal. This plant is not massive and lends itself well to use as an espalier. The foliage is distinctive against a wall.

EUONYMUS	*Celastraceae*	Winged Euonymus

E. alatus, from northeast Asia to central China, introduced about 1860, is a flat-topped deciduous shrub, broader than it is high. Height as an espalier—3 to 15 feet. Leaf—light to medium green, long tapering at the base, 3 inches long, slightly over 1 inch wide, rose-red in autumn. The winged twigs have a sculptured effect and add winter interest. Fruit —small, red, resembling bittersweet, evident after the foliage drops.

CULTURE: Zone 3b. Sun to shade. Soil—rich, light or heavy. Easily transplanted.

Uses: Informal. In winter the corky, winged stems on the angular branches provide a bold outline that is very effective against a wall, especially masonry.

FICUS   *Moraceae*   Common Fig

F. carica, from western Asia, and cultivated since ancient times, is a deciduous shrub, or, in frost-free areas, a small tree. It becomes a spreading plant, as broad as it is high. Height as an espalier—6 to 15 feet. Leaf—three- to five-lobed, 4 to 8 inches long and as wide. Pear-shaped fruit, dark brownish violet when ripe.

CULTURE: Zone 6b. Sun. Soil—light, kept evenly moist through dry seasons. An overly rich soil will delay fruit production. In northern areas, locate against a south wall to give protection from wind and cold. Withstands pruning well, so that size can be restricted by early spring trimming.

Uses: Formal or informal and for tub. The fig leaf is decorative and creates a bold pattern against stone, brick or

TWO FORSYTHIAS TRAINED IN HORIZONTAL CORDONS TRANSFORM A PLAIN HOUSE WALL TO A THING OF BEAUTY.   (*Paul E. Genereux*)

wood paneling. The branch structure gives a strong pattern in winter. Ripened fruit is a delectable treat.

FORSYTHIA	*Oleaceae*	Showy Border Forsythia Fortune Weeping Forsythia

F. intermedia spectabilis, the showy border forsythia, is a hybrid between *F. suspensa* and *F. viridissima,* both native to China. It is a deciduous shrub of arching habit. Height as an espalier—6 to 15 feet. Leaf—sharply sawtoothed, 3 inches long, 1½ inches wide, medium green. Flowers—bright yellow, mid-April. Good selections include Spring Glory (light yellow flowers in abundance) and Beatrix Farrand (very large flowers of dark yellow).

CULTURE: Zone 5b. Sun. Soil—light to heavy. Easily transplanted, grows rapidly, and pests are not troublesome.

USES: Formal or informal. Usually this spreading shrub is too large for the home garden, but as an espalier it is excellent.

F. suspensa fortunei, the Fortune weeping forsythia, was introduced about 1860 from China by Robert Fortune, an English plant explorer. It is a deciduous shrub, of arching habit with slender, pendulous stems and supple twigs. Height as an espalier—6 to 30 feet. Leaf—three-parted, the largest leaflet being 2 inches long, 1½ inch wide, light green. Flowers—yellow in mid-April, not as large or as numerous as those of the showy border forsythia.

CULTURE: Zone 5b. See *Forsythia intermedia spectabilis.*

USES: Formal or informal. This plant is almost a vine when it has a wall to serve as a support. If used in a formal pattern, branches need to be tied in place frequently.

ILEX	*Aquifoliaceae*	Burford Chinese Holly Japanese Holly Convexleaf Japanese Holly Heller Japanese Holly

I. cornuta burfordi, the Burford Chinese holly, in cultivation by 1895, is a broadleaf evergreen shrub, round-headed and dense. Height as an espalier—6 to 15 feet. Leaf—dark green, 2 to 4 inches long, very glossy, with few spines. Unlike most hollies, single plants of Burford will bear fruit. It is red and lasts all winter.

CULTURE: Zone 7b. Sun to partial shade; try to avoid a location that would subject the plant to full winter sun or strong winds. Soil—rich, well-drained, slightly acid; provide ample moisture during dry seasons. Transplant with a ball of soil.

USES: Formal or informal.

I. crenata, the Japanese holly, introduced in 1864 from Japan, is a broadleaf evergreen shrub of moderately dense, upright growth. Height as an espalier—10 to 30 feet. Leaf—elliptical, 1 inch long, half as wide, dark green, slightly glossy and without spines. Fruit—small, black, inconspicuous. The plant resembles boxwood more than traditional holly.

CULTURE: Zone 6b. Shade to sun. Soil—rich, well-drained, evenly moist. This holly is relatively easy to grow, but severe winters may damage young plants, or those near a windy corner of a building or in an open garden. Seldom troubled by pests.

USES: Formal or informal. The upright habit and the small twigs and foliage make this holly ideal in narrow, vertical places, and as a broad, fan-shaped espalier.

I. crenata convexa, the convexleaf Japanese holly, introduced in 1919 from Japan, is a broadleaf evergreen shrub, twice as wide as it is high. Height as an espalier—3 to 15 feet. Leaf —¾-inch long, less than ½-inch wide, convex- or cup-shaped, and very glossy. Hardier than boxwood and often used as a substitute.

CULTURE: Zone 6a. See *Ilex crenata.*

Uses: See *Ilex crenata*. Dark, glossy leaves of *I. c. convexa* are closely grouped and make it a refined and distinctive espalier.

I. crenata helleri, the Heller Japanese holly, originated in a Newport, Rhode Island, nursery prior to 1936, is a broadleaf evergreen shrub, low and wide-spreading, stiffly-branched, dense and flat-topped. Height as an espalier—1 to 4 feet. Leaf—less than ½-inch long, ¼-inch wide, dark green with slight glossiness.

Culture: Zone 6b. See *Ilex crenata*.

Uses: Formal or informal. The small leaf and dwarf character of this holly make it excellent as a small espalier.

JASMINUM	*Oleaceae*	Winter Jasmine

J. nudiflorum, introduced in 1844 from China, is a deciduous vinelike shrub of slender pendulous twigs. Height as an espalier—6 to 15 feet. Leaf—dark green, made up of three leaflets, the largest of which is ¾-inch long and about ¼-inch wide. There are few side branches, so that there are not many leaves on the plant. Stems—green, even in older wood. Flowers—yellow, ¾-inch in diameter, early April, or whenever the first warm spell of several days occurs toward the end of winter. In northern limits, flower buds will be damaged by cold weather before leaf buds are affected.

Culture: Zone 6. Partial shade to sun. Soil—light and well-drained. If early flowers are wanted, plant in a sunny place.

Uses: Informal. Slender twigs make this useful as a delicate tracery espalier against a wall. Treated in this manner, it is a much neater plant than the mass of jumbled twigs that develop from a standard tip-rooting, vigorous specimen plant in the open.

JUNIPERUS	*Pinaceae*	Sargent Juniper
		Andorra Juniper

J. chinensis sargenti, the Sargent juniper, introduced from Japan in 1892, is a low-spreading needle evergreen shrub. Height as an espalier—1 to 4 feet. Foliage—flat, overlapping, and appressed; the blue-green needles appear as a dense mass on individual branches. The stems are not as heavily branched as are many other spreading junipers. Blue-green berries. Hetz juniper (*J. c. hetzi*) resembles the common Pfitzer juniper but its foliage has a bluish cast. Also, it is faster growing and it has long arching branches that lend themselves to informal espalier training.

Culture: Zone 4. Sun. Soil—rich or light. Transplant with a ball of soil in the spring. This juniper is at its best in

COMMON PFITZER JUNIPER ESPALIERED ON REDWOOD FRAME AGAINST BAMBOO FENCE ADDS INTEREST NEAR ENTRYWAY TO ORIENTAL GARDEN.
(*Larry Nicholson*)

coastal areas, but should not be exposed to salt spray. It will grow in a variety of soils but is slow to become established. For this reason, it is not commonly grown by nurserymen. Red-spider may prove troublesome.

Uses: Informal or in a tub.

J. horizontalis plumosa, the Andorra juniper, is a variant of the Bar Harbor juniper (*J. horizontalis*). It was discovered at the Andorra Nursery of Pennsylvania in 1907, in a group of seedling junipers collected in Maine. Low-spreading, short vertical branches give a plumelike effect to this needle evergreen shrub. Height as an espalier—1 to 4 feet. Needles— up to ¼-inch long, flat, pointed, arranged on all sides of the twig at an acute angle. The color is medium green in summer, turning to smoky purple in colder months. Wilton or blue rug juniper (*J. h. wiltoni*) hugs the ground closely, is a blue-green color which it retains at all seasons.

Culture: Zone 3. Sun; it will die out if other shrubs spread over and give constant shade. Soil—light to heavy. Transplant with a ball of soil in spring. Red-spider and juniper blight may be troublesome. This is the most vigorous and widely grown of the spreading junipers.

Uses: Informal or in a tub. The plume foliage of this plant makes it useful for softening harsh structural lines of a building.

LABURNUM	*Leguminosae*	Waterer Goldenchain

L. watereri is a deciduous, small tree with erect or ascending branches, sparsely arranged so that the effect is light and strongly upright. Height as an espalier—10 to 30 feet. Leaf —trifoliate, each about 1½ inches long, less than 1 inch wide. The young wood is greenish brown and gives winter interest. Flowers—bright yellow, arranged in long clusters, in late May. This is a hybrid that originated prior to 1864 between *L. anagyroides* and *L. alpinum,* both native to Europe. Sometimes listed as *L. vossi.*

CULTURE: Zone 5b. Partial shade, as the foliage may burn if exposed to continuous strong sun. Soil—tolerant of light or heavy, but needs moisture and not too much acidity. Rarely troubled by pests.

USES: Formal, informal or in a tub. The showy flowers are much admired, but the clean-cut leaf pattern and winter color of trunk and stem are equally commendable.

MAGNOLIA	*Magnoliaceae*	Southern Magnolia Saucer Magnolia Star Magnolia

M. grandiflora, the Southern magnolia, occurs naturally from North Carolina to Florida and Texas, especially in coastal lowlands. It is a broadleaf, evergreen tree that forms a stately pyramid, retaining lower branches when in the open. Height as an espalier—10 to 30 feet. Leaf—5 to 8 inches long, less than half as wide, glossy and leathery. Flower—white, 8-inch diameter, fragrant, in late-May and occasionally in the summer. Sometimes called bull bay or evergreen magnolia.

CULTURE: Zone 7b. Sun. Soil—rich and moist. Withstands heat and some cold but not prolonged freezing weather. When grown near northern limits, place against a building for protection from strong winter winds.

USES: Formal or informal. This magnolia, of which the South is justly proud, makes an impressive espalier where a large masonry wall surface is available.

M. soulangeana, the saucer magnolia, originated in France in 1820 as a hybrid between *M. denudata* and *M. liliflora,* is a deciduous, small tree, broad rounded at maturity, broad pyramidal in earlier years, naturally low-branched. Height as an espalier—10 to 30 feet. Leaf—5 to 7 inches long, 3 to 4 inches wide, leathery, turning brown in late autumn. Flower —large, cup-shaped, in early May, usually white with outer petals of a pink or purple tone. Fruit resembles a knobby cucumber, and when ripe opens to display bright red berries that hang on filaments. Trunk and stems—light in color and interesting in the winter. The flower buds form after mid-summer, are large and hairy, and during the winter they resemble pussywillows. A number of selections have been made over the years, some of which have deep pink petals. *M. s. lennei* has a dark reddish purple petal of much substance and presents a sculptured effect. It flowers later than the type.

DWARF MAGNOLIA ST. MARY MAKES A HANDSOME ACCENT ON WALL NEAR ENTRYWAY OF HOUSE. SOUTHERN, SAUCER AND STAR MAGNOLIAS MAY BE USED SIMILARLY AS ESPALIERS.   (*Bob Grant*)

CULTURE: Zone 5b. Sun. Soil—rich and slightly acid. Do not plant in lowlands subject to late spring frosts. Transplant with a ball of soil in the spring, as the fleshy root is difficult to move at other times. Withstands city conditions, and is rarely troubled by pests.

USES: Formal or informal, especially effective against a stone or brick wall where the stems and leaves will make a bold appearance. Also useful in a tub.

M. stellata, the star magnolia, introduced in 1862 from Japan, is a deciduous, small tree, round-topped, that retains most of the lower branches unless pruned. Height as an espalier—6 to 30 feet. Leaf—small for a magnolia, up to 2½ inches long, and less than 1 inch wide. Flowers—white in mid-April, with fifteen or more narrow petals, fragrant. The flower bud and fruit resemble those of a saucer magnolia, but on a smaller scale. *M. s. rosea* has a deep pink flower; the variety Waterlily has smaller petals but twice as many as the type.

CULTURE: Zone 5b. Sun, soil and transplanting as for *Magnolia soulangeana.* The star magnolia is subject to a large soft scale, but is otherwise rarely troubled by pests.

USES: Formal, informal or in a tub. Attractive at all seasons and especially nice near a small home.

MALUS	*Rosaceae*	Carmine Crab Apple Dorothea Crab Apple Red Jade Crab Apple

M. atrosanguinea, the carmine crab apple, originated before 1905 from a cross between *M. halliana* and *M. sieboldi,* is a broad, round-topped, deciduous, small tree, more horizontal in habit than other crab apples. Height as an espalier—6 to 30 feet. Leaf—3 inches long, slightly more than 1 inch wide. Flower—moderately dark pink color retained from opening to petal drop, appearing annually, a characteristic not universal among the newer crab apple introductions. Fruit—less than ½ inch in diameter, not abundant or showy.

CULTURE: Zone 4. Sun. Soil—rich, light or heavy. Crab apples start to flower at an early age, are easily transplanted, and grow rapidly. No serious pests; occasionally aphids appear on new growth, but they are easily controlled.

USES: Formal, informal or in a tub. As a specimen espalier, this plant is not as striking as most of the others described. However, it is very suitable as wall or screen where a number of plants are used.

M. 'Dorothea,' a hybrid between M. halliana parkmani and M. arnoldiana, was found as a chance seedling in the Arnold Arboretum in 1943. It is a deciduous, small tree, broad and round-topped. Height as an espalier—6 to 30 feet. Leaf—2½ inches long, 1½ inches wide, medium green and slightly glossy. Flower—semidouble in two shades of rose-pink, appearing annually. Fruit—bright yellow, ½-inch in diameter. This is one of the few semidouble crab apples that produces fruit.

CULTURE: Zone 4. See Malus atrosanguinea.

USES: Formal, informal or in a tub.

M. 'Red Jade' was introduced by the Brooklyn Botanic Garden and patented in 1956. George M. Reed, the breeder at the Garden, grew thousands of seedlings and selected this one for its distinctive habit and good fruiting. It is a deciduous, small tree with long, slender, pendulous branches that give a fountain-like effect. Height as an espalier—6 to 15 feet. Leaf—3 inches long, 1½ inches wide, medium dark green. Flower—large, white. Fruit—light red, the size of a cherry, appearing in abundance, well-displayed on the pendulous branches and remaining on the tree until late fall, well after the leaves have dropped.

CULTURE: Zone 4. See M. atrosanguinea.

USES: Informal or in a tub. The habit of this tree is so

unique that it deserves to be carefully placed in the landscape as an accent.

PINUS   *Pinaceae*   Bristlecone Pine
                                                      Silver Japanese White Pine

P. aristata, the bristlecone pine, was introduced into cultivation in 1861. It occurs naturally from California to Colorado
and Arizona at high elevation. In California this plant is
found above 9,000 feet elevation. It is a needle evergreen
tree of ascending branches, densely covered with needles,
and a form that is naturally picturesque. Height as an espalier—1 to 4 feet. Needles—in bundles of five, 2 inches
long, appressed, covering the branches with a dense mat.
This tree holds its needles for twenty years—three or more
times as long as the average conifer. The needles show white
lines on the upper side and are sprinkled with white flecks of
resin, which at first glance may appear to be an infestation
of scale. This pine is a conversation piece because in recent
years specimens appearing in the White Mountains along
the California-Nevada line have been established as being
the oldest-known living things. Some are forty-five hundred
years old—fifteen hundred years older than the most vener-
able sequoia. Sometimes known as hickory pine.

CULTURE: Zone 3b. Sun. Soil—light, although this pine
is tolerant of a variety of conditions. On the West Coast it
grows in the desert as well as in the high humidity conditions
of the fog belt. It has a good root system and is easily transplanted.

USES: Formal, informal or in a tub.

P. parviflora glauca, the silver Japanese white pine, is a selection of the species introduced from Japan. It is a needle
evergreen tree of broad pyramidal form with wide spreading
branches that give a horizontal effect. The length of branches
varies, but the shape is always appealing. Height as an es-

palier—10 to 30 feet. Needles—green with a bluish cast and a white line on the upper side, 2 inches long, with five in a bundle that forms a tuftlike cluster. Short, 1½-inch cones are decorative and stay on the tree for six or seven years.

CULTURE: Zone 6a. Sun. Soil—rich or light, but always well-drained. Size can be restrained by removing the upper half of the new growth shoots, called candles.

USES: Formal or informal. The cluster of short needles, dark gray cone with its open, cuplike appendages, and the form of this tree make it excellent as a large espalier.

| PONCIRUS | *Rutaceae* | Hardy-Orange |

P. trifoliata, introduced in 1850 from northern China and Korea, is a deciduous, small tree of irregular outline. Height as an espalier—10 to 30 feet. Leaf—trifoliate, leathery and dark green, the largest leaflet being about 1½ inches long. Green thorns, broad triangular and 1½ to 2 inches long. The twigs are also green and irregularly flattened. Flower—white, 2 inches across, fragrant, in late April. Fruit—golden, up to 2 inches in diameter, like a small orange. Sometimes called the trifoliate orange.

CULTURE: Zone 6b. Sun to shade. Soil—rich, light or heavy, but preferably acid. Very tolerant of pruning.

USES: Formal or informal. Green thorns, small orange-like fruit and good foliage make this an interesting espalier.

| PRUNUS | *Rosaceae* | Amanogawa Flowering Cherry |
| | | Japanese Weeping Cherry |

P. serrulata 'Amanogawa,' the Amanogawa flowering cherry, was introduced from Japan in 1906 by David Fairchild. It is a deciduous, small tree of narrow, upright habit. Height as an espalier—20 feet. Leaf—4 to 5 inches long, about half as wide, medium light green. Flower—semidouble, light pink, 1¾ inches across. Fruit—not significant, but the foliage gives some fall color.

CULTURE: Zone 6b. Sun. Soil—rich, and evenly moist. Borers may attack the trunk; watch for them.

USES: Formal, also in a large tub. Excellent where a small, columnar tree with showy flowers is needed.

P. subhirtella pendula, the Japanese weeping cherry, was introduced in 1862 from Japan. It is a round-topped, deciduous, small tree, with slender, pendulous branches. Height as an espalier—10 to 30 feet. Leaf—3 inches long, half as wide, dark green. Flowers—single, light pink, in late April, effectively arranged on long slender twigs. Yae-shidare-higan has double flowers.

CULTURE: Zone 6b. Sun. Soil—rich, well-drained and moist. Borers may attack the trunk; watch for them.

USES: Formal, informal or in a tub. Distinctive because of early flowers and pendulous branches.

BRICK WALL OF COMMERCIAL BUILDING PROVIDES AN IDEAL SETTING FOR TWO WEEPING CHERRIES ESPALIERED AS INFORMAL FOUNTAINS. (*Patry/Carr Studios*)

PYRACANTHA   *Rosaceae*   Laland Firethorn

P. coccinea lalandi was originated about 1874 from the species native from Italy to western Asia. It is a broadleaf evergreen shrub of dense, irregular outline. Height as an espalier —6 to 30 feet. Leaf—1½ inches long, ½-inch wide, dark green, turning brown in late winter after severe cold. New leaves replace old ones in early spring. Half-inch spines. Flowers—white, appearing in a cluster, mid-June. Fruit— bright masses of orange berries, often providing color until late January.

PYRACANTHA (FIRETHORN) TRAINED IN HORIZONTAL CORDONS ON BRICK GARDEN WALL MAKES A BRIGHT DISPLAY ALL YEAR. THE BRANCHES ARE TRAINED BY MEANS OF WIRES ATTACHED TO BRICK.
(*Max Tatch*)

CULTURE: Zone 5b. Sun to shade. Soil—rich or light, but always well-drained. The firethorn is deep-rooted and transplants best when small. Withstands pruning very well. Apple scab is troublesome in some areas, and if present, results in black fruit. Lace bug may also need curtailment.

Uses: Formal, informal or in a tub. Pyracantha is one of the most widely used espaliers. It is rapid-growing, and can be trained to almost any pattern or design.

STEWARTIA	*Theaceae*	Korean Stewartia

S. koreana, introduced in 1917 from Korea, is a deciduous, small tree of upright habit forming a broad oval shape. Height as an espalier—15 to 30 feet. Leaf—3 inches long, 1¾ inches wide, medium green. In autumn the foliage makes a mosaic of blending shades, primarily orange and red, speckled with dark spots. Flower—white, 3 inches in diameter, July. The smooth trunk flakes, displaying a subtle blend of pale green, light brown and dark gray. This is one of the few trees that flowers in the summer. Sometimes called false camellia, *S. ovata grandiflora* has a more distinctive flower because of purple stamens, but the leaves do not assume showy fall coloration.

Culture: Zone 6a. Sun to shade. Soil—rich, acid, with ample humus. Provide moisture during seasons of drought. Try to select a sunny spot protected from winter winds.

Uses: Informal.

TAMARIX	*Tamaricaceae*	Five-Stamen Tamarix

T. pentandra, brought into cultivation in 1883, from southeastern Europe to central Asia, is a deciduous shrub of arching habit with slender branches. Height as an espalier—10 to 30 feet. Leaf—bluish green, ⅛-inch long, slender, needle-like. Flowers—light pink in a fluffy cluster beginning in mid-July for an extended period. The fine texture of this plant's leaf and flower makes it difficult to combine well with others. The small-flowered tamarix (*T. parviflora*) is similar but it flowers in late May and is not as hardy.

Culture: Zone 3. Sun. Soil—light or heavy. Grows rapidly, requires a considerable amount of pruning to maintain neatness. Withstands seaside conditions and is rarely troubled by pests.

USES: Informal.

TAXUS	*Taxaceae*	Spreading English Yew
		Dwarf Japanese Yew
		Hicks Yew
		Ward Yew

T. baccata repandens, spreading English yew, was brought to Highland Park, Rochester, New York, in 1911. The species is native to Europe, North Africa, and western Asia, and has been in cultivation since ancient times. This is a needle evergreen shrub, more or less flat-topped, with arching branches. Height as an espalier—1 to 8 feet. Needles—1 inch long, pointed, black-green, the darkest of yews.

CULTURE: Zone 5b. Sun to shade. Soil—rich, or light, but preferably sandy and well-drained. Partial shade is desirable although this plant will grow in deep shade. Takes pruning very well. Transplant with a ball of soil.

USES: Informal, especially good on a low wall.

T. cuspidata nana, dwarf Japanese yew, is a needle evergreen shrub, wide-spreading, irregularly flat-topped. It is one of the oldest clones of Japanese yew in cultivation. Height as an espalier—1 to 8 feet. Needles—½- to ¾-inch long, and less than ½-inch wide. The needles are shorter and more closely placed than those of the original species. Sometimes incorrectly listed as *P. brevifolia,* a name reserved for the Pacific yew native to British Columbia and milder sections of the Pacific Northwest.

CULTURE: Zone 5. Sun to partial shade. Soil—rich, well-drained and not too acid. Excessive watering on heavy soils or too deep planting will be fatal. Withstands city conditions better than other conifers. Nursery-grown plants that have been root-pruned transplant well with a ball of soil in the spring, summer or fall. Few plants could stand pruning better, and this is done as new growth develops in early summer. Generally free of pests, but black vine weevil and a soft scale may need attention.

Uses: Formal, informal or in a tub. The supple branches and dark, short needles are effective against a light-colored wall. Slow growth and small size offer distinct advantages for minimum maintenance.

T. media hicksi, the Hicks yew, selected from a group of seedlings at Hicks Nursery, Long Island, New York, about 1900, is a needle evergreen shrub of upright form with several leaders. Height as an espalier—6 to 15 feet. Needles—dark, glossy green, 1 inch long. Ascending branches with needles on four sides of the twigs. Abundant fruit. *T. m.* 'Meadowbrook' resembles the Hicks yew but has smaller needles, more closely placed on the branch. It makes a plant that is fuller to the base and more compact at the top, a recent introduction with a promising future.

Culture: Zone 6. See *Taxus cuspidata nana.*

Uses: Formal or informal. This is a favorite of some nurserymen for espalier training.

T. media wardi, the Ward yew, of garden origin, is a needle evergreen shrub with an open top, irregular in shape and dense. Height as an espalier—1 to 8 feet. Needles—less than 1 inch long, and 1/16-inch wide, dark green. The stems are covered with foliage and give a compact appearance.

Culture: Zone 6. Sun to partial shade. Soil—rich and well-drained, preferably sandy. Withstands pruning very well. Transplant with a ball of soil.

Uses: Formal, informal or in a tub. This is a compact plant, but with an irregularity in outline of the upper branches; excellent as an espalier.

VIBURNUM	*Caprifoliaceae*	Japanese Snowball
		Doublefile Viburnum
		Blackhaw Viburnum
		Siebold Viburnum

V. plicatum, the Japanese snowball, was introduced in 1814 from China and Japan. It is a deciduous shrub with an irregularly rounded head, not as wide-spreading as the doublefile viburnum. Height as an espalier—6 to 10 feet. Leaf—3½ inches long, 2¼ inches wide, dark green, rugose. Flowers—white and double, the much admired snowball type. Formerly listed as *V. tomentosum plicatum* and *V. t. sterile.*

CULTURE: Zone 6a. Sun to shade, although more floriferous in a bright location. Soil—rich or light. This plant is not subject to aphids as is the once widely planted European snowball (*V. opulus sterile*).

USES: Formal or informal. Valued for excellent foliage, and showy, long-lasting flowers.

V. plicatum tomentosum, the doublefile viburnum, was introduced about 1865, from China and Japan. It is a deciduous shrub, broad-spreading with stratification produced by horizontal branches. Height as an espalier—6 to 15 feet. Leaf—2 to 4 inches long, 1 to 2½ inches wide, dark green, rugose, bronzy red in autumn. The leaf petiole is reddish. Flowers—white in a large flat cluster with showy sterile flowers around the edge. Numerous bright red berries appear in early summer; the red petiole persists for some time. *V. p. t. mariesi* has a larger flower head.

CULTURE: Zone 5b. Otherwise see *V. plicatum.* Transplants readily, grows rapidly and is rarely troubled by pests.

USES: Best as an informal, rugged espalier for a large wall. Little if any support required.

V. prunifolium, the blackhaw viburnum, introduced in 1727, occurs naturally from Connecticut to Georgia and west to Arkansas. It is a deciduous shrub, sometimes treelike and irregularly round-headed, with some short, stout branches. Height as an espalier—10 to 20 feet. Leaf—2½ inches long, 1½ inches wide, dark green, smooth and semiglossy, turning to dark plum-red in autumn.

CULTURE: Zone 3b. Sun. Soil—rich or light, well-drained. Foliage looks fresh even when subjected to dry conditions. Will grow in partial shade, but the best plants are found in sunny positions. Transplants readily, is rarely troubled by pests, and does not grow rapidly.

USES: Formal or informal. This viburnum lends itself to horizontal training. Excellent foliage in summer and rugged winter appearance give all-year interest.

V. sieboldi, the Siebold viburnum, was introduced from Japan in 1880. It is a deciduous shrub of stiff, stout branches. Height as an espalier—10 to 30 feet. Leaf—2 to 5 inches long, 1½ to 3 inches wide, light green, thick, deeply rugose, held late with little change of color. Flowers—creamy white in a flat cluster, late in May. Fruit—cluster of berries ripening in summer and changing in color from green to bright red to black. The berries are held on red petioles, spaced in such a way that each is set off as an individual.

CULTURE: Zone 5. Sun to partial shade. Soil—light or heavy, evenly moist. Transplants readily and is rarely troubled by pests.

USES: Formal or informal. The bold foliage looks best against a large masonry structure.

SECTION 3—READY REFERENCE LISTS OF ESPALIER PLANTS

Espaliers by Height

DWARF ESPALIERS—1 TO 4 FEET

Cotoneaster horizontalis	rock cotoneaster
Ilex crenata helleri	Heller Japanese holly
Juniperus chinensis sargenti	Sargent juniper

Juniperus horizontalis plumosa	Andorra juniper
Pinus aristata	bristlecone pine
Taxus baccata repandens	spreading English yew
Taxus cuspidata nana	dwarf Japanese yew
Taxus media wardi	Ward yew

Low Espaliers—3 to 8 feet

Acer palmatum ornatum	spiderleaf Japanese maple
Arctostaphylos uva-ursi	bearberry
Cercis chinensis	Chinese redbud
Chaenomeles lagenaria	flowering quince
Cotoneaster divaricata	spreading cotoneaster
Cotoneaster francheti	Franchet cotoneaster
Euonymus alatus	winged euonymus
Ilex crenata convexa	convexleaf Japanese holly
Taxus baccata repandens	spreading English yew
Taxus cuspidata nana	dwarf Japanese yew
Taxus media wardi	Ward yew

Medium Espaliers—6 to 15 feet

Arctostaphylos uva-ursi	bearberry
Caragana arborescens lorbergi	Lorberg Siberian pea-tree
Chaenomeles lagenaria	flowering quince
Corylus maxima purpurea	purpleleaf filbert
Cotoneaster divaricata	spreading cotoneaster
Cotoneaster francheti	Franchet cotoneaster
Cotoneaster salicifolia floccosa	hardy willowleaf cotoneaster
Euonymus alatus	winged euonymus
Ficus carica	common fig
Forsythia intermedia spectabilis	showy border forsythia
Forsythia suspensa fortunei	Fortune weeping forsythia
Ilex cornuta burfordi	Burford Chinese holly

Ilex crenata convexa	convexleaf Japanese holly
Jasminum nudiflorum	winter jasmine
Magnolia stellata	star magnolia
Malus atrosanguinea	carmine crab apple
Malus 'Dorothea'	Dorothea crab apple
Malus 'Red Jade'	Red Jade crab apple
Pyracantha coccinea lalandi	Laland firethorn
Taxus media hicksi	Hicks yew
Viburnum plicatum	Japanese snowball
Viburnum plicatum tomentosum	doublefile viburnum

TALL ESPALIERS—10 TO 30 FEET

Acer palmatum atropurpureum	bloodleaf Japanese maple
Camellia japonica	Japanese camellia
Caragana arborescens lorbergi	Lorberg Siberian pea-tree
Cedrus atlantica glauca	blue Atlas cedar
Cercis canadensis alba	white redbud
Chaenomeles sinensis	Chinese quince
Cornus kousa	Japanese dogwood
Corylus maxima purpurea	purpleleaf filbert
Cotoneaster salicifolia floccosa	hardy willowleaf cotoneaster
Forsythia suspensa fortunei	Fortune weeping forsythia
Ilex crenata	Japanese holly
Laburnum watereri	Waterer goldenchain
Magnolia grandiflora	Southern magnolia
Magnolia soulangeana	saucer magnolia
Magnolia stellata	star magnolia
Malus atrosanguinea	carmine crab apple
Malus 'Dorothea'	Dorothea crab apple
Pinus parviflora glauca	silver Japanese white pine
Poncirus trifoliata	hardy-orange

Prunus serrulata 'Amanogawa'	Amanogawa flowering cherry
Prunus subhirtella pendula	Japanese weeping cherry
Pyracantha coccinea lalandi	Laland firethorn
Stewartia koreana	Korean stewartia
Tamarix pentandra	five-stamen tamarix
Viburnum prunifolium	blackhaw viburnum
Viburnum sieboldi	Siebold viburnum

Espaliers According to Hardiness

Based on 1960 USDA Zone of Hardiness Map—see end-papers of this book: *a* indicates above average hardiness for the zone; *b* indicates that the plant is more tender than the average for the zone. An espalier cold-hardy in Zone 3 obviously would be cold-hardy in the balance of the zones given in this book, that is 4 through 7. Therefore, the person who lives in Zone 7 may choose from all plants listed, while the person who lives in Zone 3 is limited to only a few. The person who lives in Zone 5 could grow all the plants listed in that zone, plus those in zones 3 and 4, but probably none of those listed for zones 6 and 7. (See page 40 also.)

ZONE 3: −40 TO −30 DEGREES

Arctostaphylos uva-ursi	bearberry
Caragana arborescens lorbergi	Lorberg Siberian pea-tree
Euonymus alatus (b)	winged euonymus
Juniperus horizontalis plumosa	Andorra juniper
Pinus aristata (b)	bristlecone pine
Tamarix pentandra	five-stamen tamarix
Viburnum prunifolium (b)	blackhaw viburnum

ZONE 4: −30 TO −20 DEGREES

Juniperus chinensis sargenti	Sargent juniper

Malus atrosanguinea	carmine crab apple
Malus 'Dorothea'	Dorothea crab apple
Malus 'Red Jade'	Red Jade crab apple

ZONE 5: −20 TO −10 DEGREES

Cercis canadensis alba (b)	white redbud
Chaenomeles lagenaria	flowering quince
Cornus kousa (b)	Japanese dogwood
Cornus mas	Cornelian cherry
Corylus maxima purpurea	purpleleaf filbert
Cotoneaster divaricata (b)	spreading cotoneaster
Forsythia intermedia spectabilis (b)	showy border forsythia
Forsythia suspensa fortunei (b)	Fortune weeping forsythia
Laburnum watererei (b)	Waterer goldenchain
Magnolia soulangeana (b)	saucer magnolia
Magnolia stellata (b)	star magnolia
Pyracantha coccinea lalandi (b)	Laland firethorn
Taxus baccata repandens (b)	spreading English yew
Taxus cuspidata nana	dwarf Japanese yew
Viburnum plicatum tomentosum (b)	doublefile viburnum
Viburnum sieboldi	Siebold viburnum

ZONE 6: −10 TO 0 DEGREES

Acer palmatum atropurpureum (a)	bloodleaf Japanese maple
Acer palmatum ornatum (a)	spiderleaf Japanese maple
Cercis chinensis (b)	Chinese redbud
Chaenomeles sinensis	Chinese quince
Cotoneaster francheti	Franchet cotoneaster
Cotoneaster horizontalis	rock cotoneaster

Cotoneaster salicifolia floccosa (b)	hardy willowleaf cotoneaster
Ficus carica (b)	common fig
Ilex crenata (b)	Japanese holly
Ilex crenata convexa (a)	convexleaf Japanese holly
Ilex crenata helleri (b)	Heller Japanese holly
Jasminum nudiflorum	winter jasmine
Pinus parviflora glauca (a)	silver Japanese white pine
Poncirus trifoliata (b)	hardy-orange
Prunus serrulata 'Amano-gawa' (b)	Amanogawa flowering cherry
Prunus subhirtella pendula (b)	Japanese weeping cherry
Stewartia koreana (a)	Korean stewartia
Taxus media hicksi	Hicks yew
Taxus media wardi	Ward yew
Viburnum plicatum (a)	Japanese snowball

ZONE 7: 0 TO 10 DEGREES

Camellia japonica	Japanese camellia
Camellia sasanqua (b)	sasanqua camellia
Cedrus atlantica glauca (a)	blue Atlas cedar
Ilex cornuta burfordi (b)	Burford Chinese holly
Magnolia grandiflora (b)	Southern magnolia

Espaliers and Architecture

FOR ONE-STORY BUILDINGS

Acer palmatum atropurpureum	bloodleaf Japanese maple
Acer palmatum ornatum	spiderleaf Japanese maple
Camellia japonica	Japanese camellia
Cercis canadensis alba	white redbud
Cercis chinensis	Chinese redbud
Corylus maxima purpurea	purpleleaf filbert
Cotoneaster divaricata	spreading cotoneaster

Cotoneaster francheti	Franchet cotoneaster
Cotoneaster horizontalis	rock cotoneaster
Cotoneaster salicifolia floccosa	hardy willowleaf cotoneaster
Ilex cornuta burfordi	Burford Chinese holly
Ilex crenata convexa	convexleaf Japanese holly
Ilex crenata helleri	Heller Japanese holly
Jasminum nudiflorum	winter jasmine
Juniperus chinensis sargenti	Sargent juniper
Juniperus horizontalis plumosa	Andorra juniper
Magnolia stellata	star magnolia
Pinus aristata	bristlecone pine
Poncirus trifoliata	hardy-orange
Prunus subhirtella pendula	Japanese weeping cherry
Pyracantha coccinea lalandi	Laland firethorn
Taxus baccata repandens	spreading English yew
Taxus cuspidata nana	dwarf Japanese yew
Taxus media wardi	Ward yew
Viburnum plicatum	Japanese snowball

FOR MULTISTORY BUILDINGS

Acer palmatum atropurpureum	bloodleaf Japanese maple
Camellia japonica	Japanese camellia
Caragana arborescens lorbergi	Lorberg Siberian pea-tree
Cedrus atlantica glauca	blue Atlas cedar
Cercis canadensis alba	white redbud
Cercis chinensis	Chinese redbud
Chaenomeles lagenaria	flowering quince
Chaenomeles sinensis	Chinese quince
Cornus kousa	Japanese dogwood
Cornus mas	Cornelian cherry

Corylus maxima purpurea	purpleleaf filbert
Cotoneaster divaricata	spreading cotoneaster
Cotoneaster francheti	Franchet cotoneaster
Cotoneaster horizontalis	rock cotoneaster
Cotoneaster salicifolia floccosa	hardy willowleaf cotoneaster
Euonymus alatus	winged euonymus
Ficus carica	common fig
Forsythia intermedia spectabilis	showy border forsythia
Forsythia suspensa fortunei	Fortune weeping forsythia
Ilex crenata	Japanese holly
Ilex crenata convexa	convexleaf Japanese holly
Laburnum watereri	Waterer goldenchain
Magnolia grandiflora	Southern magnolia
Magnolia soulangeana	saucer magnolia
Magnolia stellata	star magnolia
Malus atrosanguinea	carmine crab apple
Malus 'Dorothea'	Dorothea crab apple
Malus 'Red Jade'	Red Jade crab apple
Pinus parviflora glauca	silver Japanese white pine
Poncirus trifoliata	hardy-orange
Prunus serrulata 'Amanogawa'	Amanogawa flowering cherry
Prunus subhirtella pendula	Japanese weeping cherry
Pyracantha coccinea lalandi	Laland firethorn
Stewartia koreana	Korean stewartia
Tamarix pentandra	five-stamen tamarix
Taxus media hicksi	Hicks yew
Viburnum plicatum	Japanese snowball
Viburnum plicatum tomentosum	doublefile viburnum
Viburnum prunifolium	blackhaw viburnum
Viburnum sieboldi	Siebold viburnum

For Contemporary Styles

Contemporary architecture, even though a building is only one story high, calls for special treatment of the large, undecorated wall surfaces. Espaliers for this use need to be bold in foliage and branch structure. In addition, those with colorful foliage—red, yellow or gray in summer—are listed for this use because their appearance is in keeping with massive structures. They may be difficult to use, but this makes their proper use all the more challenging and interesting.

Camellia japonica	Japanese camellia
Cedrus atlantica glauca	blue Atlas cedar
Cercis chinensis	Chinese redbud
Chaenomeles sinensis	Chinese quince
Cornus kousa	Japanese dogwood
Cornus mas	Cornelian cherry
Corylus maxima purpurea	purpleleaf filbert
Cotoneaster divaricata	spreading cotoneaster
Cotoneaster horizontalis	rock cotoneaster
Cotoneaster salicifolia floccosa	hardy willowleaf cotoneaster
Euonymus alatus	winged euonymus
Ficus carica	common fig
Ilex cornuta burfordi	Burford Chinese holly
Ilex crenata	Japanese holly
Ilex crenata convexa	convexleaf Japanese holly
Ilex crenata helleri	Heller Japanese holly
Juniperus chinensis sargenti	Sargent juniper
Laburnum watereri	Waterer goldenchain
Magnolia grandiflora	Southern magnolia
Magnolia soulangeana	saucer magnolia
Magnolia stellata	star magnolia
Malus 'Red Jade'	Red Jade crab apple

Pinus aristata	bristlecone pine
Pinus parviflora glauca	silver Japanese white pine
Poncirus trifoliata	hardy-orange
Prunus serrulata 'Amanogawa'	Amanogawa flowering cherry
Pyracantha coccinea lalandi	Laland firethorn
Stewartia koreana	Korean stewartia
Taxus baccata repandens	spreading English yew
Taxus cuspidata nana	dwarf Japanese yew
Taxus media hicksi	Hicks yew
Taxus media wardi	Ward yew
Viburnum plicatum	Japanese snowball
Viburnum plicatum tomentosum	doublefile viburnum
Viburnum prunifolium	blackhaw viburnum
Viburnum sieboldi	Siebold viburnum

ESPALIERS FOR CITY GARDENS

Cercis chinensis	Chinese redbud
Euonymus alatus	winged euonymus
Ficus carica	common fig
Forsythia intermedia spectabilis	showy border forsythia
Forsythia suspensa fortunei	Fortune weeping forsythia
Ilex cornuta burfordi	Burford Chinese holly
Ilex crenata	Japanese holly
Ilex crenata convexa	convexleaf Japanese holly
Pinus aristata	bristlecone pine
Pinus parviflora glauca	silver Japanese white pine
Taxus baccata repandens	spreading English yew
Taxus cuspidata nana	dwarf Japanese yew
Taxus media hicksi	Hicks yew
Taxus media wardi	Ward yew
Viburnum plicatum	Japanese snowball

Viburnum plicatum tomentosum	doublefile viburnum
Viburnum prunifolium	blackhaw viburnum

ESPALIERS FOR SEASIDE GARDENS

Acer palmatum atropurpureum	bloodleaf Japanese maple
Acer palmatum ornatum	spiderleaf Japanese maple
Caragana arborescens lorbergi	Lorberg Siberian pea-tree
Cedrus atlantica glauca	blue Atlas cedar
Cotoneaster francheti	Franchet cotoneaster
Cotoneaster horizontalis	rock cotoneaster
Cotoneaster salicifolia floccosa	hardy willowleaf cotoneaster
Ilex cornuta burfordi	Burford Chinese holly
Ilex crenata	Japanese holly
Ilex crenata convexa	convexleaf Japanese holly
Ilex crenata helleri	Heller Japanese holly
Juniperus chinensis sargenti	Sargent juniper
Juniperus horizontalis plumosa	Andorra juniper
Pinus aristata	bristlecone pine
Pinus parviflora glauca	silver Japanese white pine
Prunus serrulata 'Amanogawa'	Amanogawa flowering cherry
Prunus subhirtella pendula	Japanese weeping cherry
Pyracantha coccinea lalandi	Laland firethorn
Tamarix pentandra	five-stamen tamarix
Taxus baccata repandens	spreading English yew
Taxus cuspidata nana	dwarf Japanese yew
Taxus media hicksi	Hicks yew
Taxus media wardi	Ward yew
Viburnum plicatum	Japanese snowball

Viburnum plicatum tomentosum	doublefile viburnum
Viburnum prunifolium	blackhaw viburnum
Viburnum sieboldi	Siebold viburnum

Espaliers for Special Effects

With Foliage Attractive in Summer

Acer palmatum atropurpureum	bloodleaf Japanese maple
Acer palmatum ornatum	spiderleaf Japanese maple
Camellia japonica	Japanese camellia
Caragana arborescens lorbergi	Lorberg Siberian pea-tree
Cedrus atlantica glauca	blue Atlas cedar
Chaenomeles lagenaria	flowering quince
Chaenomeles sinensis	Chinese quince
Cornus mas	Cornelian cherry
Corylus maxima purpurea	purpleleaf filbert
Cotoneaster divaricata	spreading cotoneaster
Cotoneaster francheti	Franchet cotoneaster
Cotoneaster horizontalis	rock cotoneaster
Cotoneaster salicifolia floccosa	hardy willowleaf cotoneaster
Ficus carica	common fig
Ilex cornuta burfordi	Burford Chinese holly
Ilex crenata	Japanese holly
Ilex crenata convexa	convexleaf Japanese holly
Ilex crenata helleri	Heller Japanese holly
Juniperus chinensis sargenti	Sargent juniper
Juniperus horizontalis plumosa	Andorra juniper
Laburnum watereri	Waterer goldenchain
Magnolia grandiflora	Southern magnolia
Magnolia soulangeana	saucer magnolia
Magnolia stellata	star magnolia

Pinus parviflora glauca	silver Japanese white pine
Poncirus trifoliata	hardy-orange
Taxus baccata repandens	spreading English yew
Taxus cuspidata nana	dwarf Japanese yew
Taxus media hicksi	Hicks yew
Taxus media wardi	Ward yew
Viburnum plicatum	Japanese snowball
Viburnum plicatum tomentosum	doublefile viburnum
Viburnum prunifolium	blackhaw viburnum
Viburnum sieboldi	Siebold viburnum

Colorful Foliage for Autumn

Acer palmatum atropurpureum	bloodleaf Japanese maple
Acer palmatum ornatum	spiderleaf Japanese maple
Chaenomeles sinensis	Chinese quince
Cornus kousa	Japanese dogwood
Cotoneaster divaricata	spreading cotoneaster
Cotoneaster francheti	Franchet cotoneaster
Cotoneaster salicifolia floccosa	hardy willowleaf cotoneaster
Euonymus alatus	winged euonymus
Juniperus horizontalis plumosa	Andorra juniper
Prunus serrulata 'Amanogawa'	Amanogawa flowering cherry
Stewartia koreana	Korean stewartia
Viburnum plicatum	Japanese snowball
Viburnum plicatum tomentosum	doublefile viburnum
Viburnum prunifolium	blackhaw viburnum

For Spring Flowers

Camellia japonica	Japanese camellia

Caragana arborescens lorbergi	Lorberg Siberian pea-tree
Cercis canadensis alba	white redbud
Cercis chinensis	Chinese redbud
Chaenomeles lagenaria	flowering quince
Chaenomeles sinensis	Chinese quince
Cornus mas	Cornelian cherry
Corylus maxima purpurea	purpleleaf filbert
Forsythia intermedia spectabilis	showy border forsythia
Forsythia suspensa fortunei	Fortune weeping forsythia
Jasminum nudiflorum	winter jasmine
Laburnum watereri	Waterer goldenchain
Magnolia grandiflora	Southern magnolia
Magnolia soulangeana	saucer magnolia
Magnolia stellata	star magnolia
Malus atrosanguinea	carmine crab apple
Malus 'Dorothea'	Dorothea crab apple
Malus 'Red Jade'	Red Jade crab apple
Poncirus trifoliata	hardy-orange
Prunus serrulata 'Amanogawa'	Amanogawa flowering cherry
Prunus subhirtella pendula	Japanese weeping cherry
Viburnum plicatum	Japanese snowball
Viburnum plicatum tomentosum	doublefile viburnum
Viburnum prunifolium	blackhaw viburnum

For Summer Flowers

Cornus kousa	Japanese dogwood
Stewartia koreana	Korean stewartia
Tamarix pentandra	five-stamen tamarix

With Ornamental Fruits

Cotoneaster divaricata	spreading cotoneaster

Cotoneaster francheti	Franchet cotoneaster
Cotoneaster horizontalis	rock cotoneaster
Ficus carica	common fig
Ilex cornuta burfordi	Burford Chinese holly
Malus 'Dorothea'	Dorothea crab apple
Malus 'Red Jade'	Red Jade crab apple
Poncirus trifoliata	hardy-orange
Pyracantha coccinea lalandi	Laland firethorn
Viburnum plicatum	Japanese snowball
Viburnum plicatum tomen-tosum	doublefile viburnum
Viburnum sieboldi	Siebold viburnum

Espaliers for Special Sites

For Shade

Camellia japonica	Japanese camellia
Chaenomeles lagenaria	flowering quince
Chaenomeles sinensis	Chinese quince
Cornus mas	Cornelian cherry
Euonymus alatus	winged euonymus
Ilex crenata	Japanese holly
Ilex crenata convexa	convexleaf Japanese holly
Ilex crenata helleri	Heller Japanese holly
Laburnum watereri	Waterer goldenchain
Poncirus trifoliata	hardy-orange
Pyracantha coccinea lalandi	Laland firethorn
Stewartia koreana	Korean stewartia
Taxus baccata repandens	spreading English yew
Taxus cuspidata nana	dwarf Japanese yew
Taxus media hicksi	Hicks yew
Taxus media wardi	Ward yew
Viburnum plicatum	Japanese snowball
Viburnum plicatum tomen-tosum	doublefile viburnum

For Sun

Acer palmatum atropurpureum	bloodleaf Japanese maple
Acer palmatum ornatum	spiderleaf Japanese maple
Caragana arborescens lorbergi	Lorberg Siberian pea-tree
Cedrus atlantica glauca	blue Atlas cedar
Cercis canadensis alba	white redbud
Cercis chinensis	Chinese redbud
Chaenomeles lagenaria	flowering quince
Chaenomeles sinensis	Chinese quince
Cornus kousa	Japanese dogwood
Cornus mas	Cornelian cherry
Corylus maxima purpurea	purpleleaf filbert
Cotoneaster divaricata	spreading cotoneaster
Cotoneaster francheti	Franchet cotoneaster
Cotoneaster horizontalis	rock cotoneaster
Cotoneaster salicifolia floccosa	hardy willowleaf cotoneaster
Euonymus alatus	winged euonymus
Ficus carica	common fig
Forsythia intermedia spectabilis	showy border forsythia
Forsythia suspensa fortunei	Fortune weeping forsythia
Ilex cornuta burfordi	Burford Chinese holly
Ilex crenata	Japanese holly
Ilex crenata convexa	convexleaf Japanese holly
Ilex crenata helleri	Heller Japanese holly
Jasminum nudiflorum	winter jasmine
Juniperus chinensis sargenti	Sargent juniper
Juniperus horizontalis plumosa	Andorra juniper
Laburnum watereri	Waterer goldenchain
Magnolia grandiflora	Southern magnolia

Magnolia soulangeana	saucer magnolia
Magnolia stellata	star magnolia
Malus atrosanguinea	carmine crab apple
Malus 'Dorothea'	Dorothea crab apple
Malus 'Red Jade'	Red Jade crab apple
Pinus aristata	bristlecone pine
Pinus parviflora glauca	silver Japanese white pine
Poncirus trifoliata	hardy-orange
Prunus serrulata 'Amano-gawa'	Amanogawa flowering cherry
Prunus subhirtella pendula	Japanese weeping cherry
Pyracantha coccinea lalandi	Laland firethorn
Stewartia koreana	Korean stewartia
Tamarix pentandra	five-stamen tamarix
Taxus baccata repandens	spreading English yew
Taxus cuspidata nana	dwarf Japanese yew
Taxus media hicksi	Hicks yew
Taxus media wardi	Ward yew
Viburnum plicatum	Japanese snowball
Viburnum plicatum tomentosum	doublefile viburnum
Viburnum prunifolium	blackhaw viburnum
Viburnum sieboldi	Siebold viburnum

For Container Gardening

A plant to be espaliered in a tub or other large container needs to have a restrained root system, a refined habit of growth, commendable form at close range and at least *one* of these traits: good bloom, fruit, foliage or winter pattern.

Acer palmatum atropurpureum	bloodleaf Japanese maple
Acer palmatum ornatum	spiderleaf Japanese maple
Camellia japonica	Japanese camellia
Ficus carica	common fig

Jasminum nudiflorum	winter jasmine
Juniperus chinensis sargenti	Sargent juniper
Juniperus horizontalis plumosa	Andorra juniper
Laburnum watereri	Waterer goldenchain
Magnolia grandiflora	Southern magnolia
Magnolia soulangeana	saucer magnolia
Magnolia stellata	star magnolia
Malus atrosanguinea	carmine crab apple
Malus 'Dorothea'	Dorothea crab apple
Malus 'Red Jade'	Red Jade crab apple
Pinus aristata	bristlecone pine
Prunus serrulata 'Amanogawa'	Amanogawa flowering cherry
Prunus subhirtella pendula	Japanese weeping cherry
Pyracantha coccinea lalandi	Laland firethorn
Taxus cuspidata nana	dwarf Japanese yew
Taxus media wardi	Ward yew

Many tropical plants make excellent tub espaliers in northern gardens, provided they are kept indoors in a cool but frost-free place in winter. These include all of the citrus trees (grapefruit, kumquat, lemon, lime, orange and tangerine), loquat (*Eriobotrya japonica*), strawberry-guava (*Psidium cattleianum*), Japanese persimmon (*Diospyros* species), Chinese hibiscus (*Hibiscus rosa-sinensis*), and the common fig (*Ficus carica*) in areas where it is not winter-hardy.

6

Fruit Trees as Espaliers

A dwarf fruit tree espaliered in an attractive pattern offers particular delight to the gardener. You can have the satisfaction of growing your own fruit, and at the same time have a plant with which you can be creative. Thus the utilitarian is combined with the decorative—in the way the French have gardened for centuries.

Dwarf fruit trees espaliered take up even less space than regular dwarfs. Fruit production occurs for most varieties the second or third year after planting, well ahead of what could be expected of standard trees. Spraying can be accomplished with small equipment, and pruning and picking of fruit can be done without a ladder-balancing act.

Commercial growers must limit varieties to those that measure up to production and marketing standards. You may grow a variety only for its superb flavor. The commercial grower cannot use a type that bruises easily, bears shyly or has a subdued color without eye-appeal.

FRUIT ESPALIERS IN THE LANDSCAPE

Espalier fruit trees are valuable for landscape effects. In part, their versatility lies in the fact that they may be kept to 18 inches as a single horizontal cordon or they can be trained to 30 feet to cover one end of a multi-story building. Some kind of fan shape might be used to cover a wide wall while two-armed U-shaped plants are suited to a narrow place. The low cordons make a wonderful garden wall edging; those of intermediate height, including the lattice or Belgian fence types, can be used to separate two gardens.

ESPALIERED FRUIT TREES MAKE USEFUL AS WELL AS DECORATIVE PLANTS FOR TODAY'S SMALL GARDENS. THIS APPLE TREE IS TRAINED ON WIRES SUPPORTED BY STEEL PIPE IN NARROW SPACE BETWEEN HOUSE AND LAWN.   (*Jeannette Grossman*)

In fact, the uses of espalier dwarf fruit trees are limited only by the gardener's imagination.

PLANTING DWARF FRUIT TREES

The best way to obtain an espalier fruit tree is to buy one already started in a pattern by a specialist. Several nurserymen offer such stock. A dwarf fruit-tree espalier begins with the grafting of a selected variety onto a dwarfing rootstock.

This produces the controlled growth necessary to success. After this, a frame to which the tree can be tied is supplied, and the frame remains with the tree until it is placed in its permanent home. Even then, of course, the tree needs a wire or wooden support on which to be tied so that shape will be retained regardless of snow, wind or heavy fruit production.

A young grafted tree is grown for two to three years, with some pruning each year, before it is ready to be trained. Then a wooden frame is placed behind it, and the shaping process begins. The tree may require another four to five years, with much careful shaping and pruning, before it is ready to be sold. Some individual trees lend themselves to training in one way and some in another. Where there is a large field of young trees from which to choose, good selection can be made. A one-, two-, or three-tiered horizontal cordon, a two-, four-, or six-arm palmette, or a fan shape may be chosen. Early training is important and difficult, but many gardeners will not be satisfied until they have tried their hand at developing espaliered dwarf fruit trees. Of course, after the pattern has been set by a specialist, even a novice can retain it.

Standard apples are grafted onto seedlings, but dwarf trees result from grafting onto a special clonal rootstock that is not reproduced by seed. Malling rootstocks, selected by the famous East Malling Research Station of Kent, England, are used for apples. Malling stocks #2, #7 and #9 are most common. Some varieties are better grafted on one stock than on another. Apples grafted on Malling #2 will grow to about three-fourths the size of a standard tree. Those on #7 will be about half the standard size, and those on #9 will produce 5- to 10-foot trees, the dwarfest of all. Variations in height arise as a result of differences in soil conditions or varieties selected. The root system of Malling #9 is brittle, but since espalier fruits are fastened to supports, this problem is minimized.

Pears are grafted onto quince for dwarfing. Peaches, nectarines and plums are grafted onto *Prunus besseyi* or *P. tomentosa*. Cherries are grafted onto Mahaleb cherry seedlings or sometimes onto certain Morello cherries. The dwarfing in cherries is not as marked as in most other fruits, however.

Give some thought to pollination. Many varieties of apple and pear are self-sterile. They will either produce no fruit or give only a small crop unless another variety that blooms at the same time is present to produce pollen. Even varieties that are self-fruitful will produce a better crop when other varieties are planted nearby. Red Delicious and Cortland apples are known to be good pollinators, so one of these might be selected. Peaches and sour cherries do not require cross-pollination but they usually fruit better where more than one variety is used. Honey bees and other pollen-carrying insects act as pollinizing agents. If you have room to plant only one fruit-tree espalier, be sure to get a self-pollinator. Information on this is given in most nursery catalogs.

Choosing the Site

When you select a site for fruit trees, keep in mind that the trees need a minimum of six hours of sun to produce good fruit. They won't thrive near a large shade tree whose spreading roots take essential water and nutrients from them.

If espalier fruit trees are planted against a light-colored wall and exposed to full sun in the warmest part of the day, high temperatures may damage plant and fruit. An eastern or western exposure is preferred to a fully exposed southern one. Soil needs to be well-drained. Be sure plants are not located in a frost pocket. Cold air is heavier than warm air and will settle in these spots. Late frost at the time of spring flowering can severely damage a potential fruit crop if a tree has been improperly located. There can be several degrees difference between one part of a property and another. These few degrees are critical during the times of late spring and early autumn frosts. Cold air flows somewhat like a stream of water, and thus a solid barrier, such as a wall, fence or hedge, may stop and hold cold air just as a dam holds water. If an opening is provided in this obstruction, the cold air will flow through to a lower area.

Spring is a favorite planting time for fruit trees in areas north of New York City. South of New York, either fall or spring planting is satisfactory. Peaches and cherries that have thin bark are most sensitive to winter damage while becoming established so that spring planting is favored for them.

Planting a fruit tree is very little different from planting any other tree or shrub. It is important to look for the graft union, indicated by slight swelling of the trunk. Be sure that this is a few inches *above* the soil line. If the union is placed below, rooting will take place above the graft and the dwarfing effect will be lost.

CARE OF ESTABLISHED FRUIT ESPALIERS

Winter

Basically two types of pruning are necessary on fruit-tree espaliers: first, to keep a plant in its trained pattern and to achieve neatness; second, to promote fruit production. The first or heavier pruning is done during the dormant season when a plant is without leaves, before sap starts to flow in early spring. Apples and pears may be pruned at any time during this period, but peaches, more subject to injury, are best pruned in late winter. This pruning needs to be done every year; if neglected, the espalier fruit tree soon loses its form and distinctiveness, and these are not readily restored.

When a plant is without leaves, the structure can be studied more easily to determine where to remove or shorten a branch. It is also easier at that time to make a cut at the node, where a bud or side branch is located. Do not leave

TRAINING ESPALIER FRUIT TREES

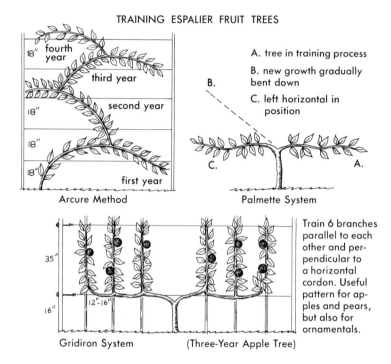

Arcure Method

A. tree in training process

B. new growth gradually bent down

C. left horizontal in position

Palmette System

Gridiron System   (Three-Year Apple Tree)

Train 6 branches parallel to each other and perpendicular to a horizontal cordon. Useful pattern for apples and pears, but also for ornamentals.

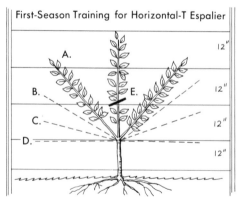

First-Season Training for Horizontal-T Espalier

A. laterals allowed to develop

B. same laterals bent down further

C. bent down still further

D. in final position

E. central leader allowed to develop; cut following spring at height of second cordon

FIGURE 6

stubs, as they are unsightly, and, even more important, a tree cannot heal over the stub by producing the usual callus growth.

Cut back the previous year's growth leaving only 6 inches of newly developed wood. When an abundance of new wood develops, some shoots may be removed completely with a flush cut to the older branch. Cordons are an exception in that the main leader is not cut back until it has reached a length sufficient to fill the space for which it was intended. On any type of espalier, after the full length or height is reached, the terminal growth is cut back leaving just one bud of currently produced wood. Older branches that are at variance with the form of the espalier may also be removed at that time.

The Belgian fence espalier will eventually develop an excess of short branches near the top. Every three years, these can be reduced in number by removing about 70 per cent of them. Make a cut to a node about 2 inches below the uppermost bud.

Spring

Spraying of the commercial orchard has become a specialized craft that requires constant study and diligent attention. Fortunately for the home orchardist, a general-purpose spray may be used that contains ingredients to control chewing and sucking insects as well as diseases. It can be applied as few as five times a year, in contrast to the twenty sprayings done by commercial orchardists every season. While this efficiency spray for the home orchardist may not give full control, it is at least 75 per cent effective.

Successful spraying depends on timing, thorough coverage and proper material. Always follow directions on the package. Many of the materials used are poisonous and need to be treated with respect. Mix only enough spray for one application and discard any that is left over. Wash out sprayer after work is completed. Keep poisonous sprays beyond the reach of children and household pets.

Spray recommendations differ, of course, for various fruits, but they also vary from year to year as new materials are introduced. There are also regional differences as to the type of pest more prevalent. For these reasons, I recommend that you consult your own county agricultural agent, the extension horticulturist at your state university or your state agricultural experiment station to find out the best general sprays for your locality. All have printed spray programs both for large commercial operators and for back-yard growers with only a few trees. These men are also in a position to recommend the best varieties of fruit trees for your particular area.

Another job in the spring is to apply a complete fertilizer to dwarf fruit trees. A fertilizer with a nitrogen, phosphorus and potassium ratio of about 5–10–5 is recommended. Avoid making heavy applications of a fertilizer with a high nitrogen content, as this will force the dwarf tree into too rapid growth. In some regions certain minor elements need to be added for success with fruit trees. The amount needed depends on the size of the tree and the natural fertility of the soil. Here, again, your local county agricultural agent can be of assistance in getting your soil tested and in making recommendations for the site.

Fruits need to be thinned in early June while they are still small; a better product will result. With plums, thinning is also an aid in disease control. An extra heavy crop in apple trees will induce a biennial bearing habit instead of the more desirable annual cropping. Apples and pears need to be spaced no closer than 6 inches, while peaches and, particularly, plums can be 3 to 4 inches apart.

Summer

Light pruning or pinching back is done in June, July or early August to help maintain an orderly-looking plant.

Since this is the period of flower bud initiation, light pruning slows down the vegetative growth and insures a future supply of fruit.

In summer pruning, new side shoots are cut back so that they are no more than 4 to 6 inches long. With the Belgian fence, the amount depends on the size of the opening to be maintained, which in turn depends on the spacing of the trees. For a smaller opening, growth may be restricted to 2 inches; with others, 4 to 6 inches is suitable.

Fruit spurs on apples or pears are to be treated with respect. These appear as stubby growth with a large bud and a cluster of leaves concentrated near the end. They take a number of years to form and have a darker color than other twigs. Here is where fruit is borne year after year. Pinching back new growth in early summer helps in the formation of fruit spurs. A proper balance of root and top is also needed; excessive pruning and heavy fertilization, both of which induce a great deal of top growth, will upset the delicate balance and delay flowering. Peaches flower on wood that was produced the previous year. For that reason, they can be more severely pruned and do not require as much horticultural skill on the part of the gardener.

Autumn

During the colder months, rabbits and mice can severely damage or kill fruit trees. Frequently the damage caused is not noticed until too late to do anything about it. Rabbits chew out the bark of the lower part of the trunk and may completely girdle it. To avoid this, in autumn, before heavy freezes occur, place a collar of ¼-inch mesh wire around the trunk of each tree, or use a cylinder made of hardware cloth 2 feet high, or up to the lower branches. In case of heavy snow, rabbit damage may occur above the protected area. Live-animal traps may be used to supplement the wire screen. Mice work on the roots just below the ground line and may girdle them. Special poison baits may be used. For detailed information about this problem in your own region, consult your county agricultural agent.

PATTERNS FOR ESPALIERED TREES

Dwarf apples and pears may be trained as cordons or by gridiron, Belgian fence or arcure method. Plums, nectarines, peaches, apricots and cherries are best trained in fan shape. Red and white currants may be trained as cordons or by Belgian fence, arcure or gridiron method. Gooseberries are best used as fans or cordons. Raspberries, blackberries and loganberries do well in fan shape. Grapes, discussed in detail in Part II of this book, are usually trained as cordons, but they might also be trained upright as informal espaliers (Figure 10).

ESPALIER FRUITS FOR CONTAINER GARDENING

Dwarf forms of apples, apricots, cherries, nectarines, peaches, pears and plums are suitable for containers. Those obtained from the nursery, either bareroot or in a small container, will probably first go to a 3- to 5-gallon tub for two to three years, then to a larger container. Finally you can allow them to mature in a tub about 20 inches in diameter.

Tubbed fruit trees need careful attention so that soil never dries out completely. They need frequent but very light feedings of fertilizer to keep growth sturdy and vigorous. Obviously, the fruit yield from a tree restricted by a container will not be appreciable, but the effect of an espaliered dwarf fruit tree in a tub is delightful. In fact, many people today use these on the terrace or patio, or in other outdoor living areas; when a tree lacks real fruit, they may attach realistic artificial fruits for special occasions.

In climates where citrus fruits are cultivated outdoors through the year, dwarf forms of grapefruit, lemon, lime, orange, tangerine, kumquat and calamondin make excellent espalier plants. The loquat, fig and strawberry-guava are also often trained as espaliers. In cold climates, all of these may be used as tub plants, kept outdoors in summer in a warm sunny location with moist soil and ample feeding, and brought to a frost-free well-lighted place during periods of the year when freezing might occur.

Part **II**

Vines for Pleasure and Purpose

7

The Right Vine for the Right Place

Vines or climbing plants have entered a new era of usefulness because of our desire to live outdoors on terrace or patio during warm seasons. The grape, classic vine for pergolas or arbors, is enjoying unprecedented favor in some sections of the country for use with modern architecture, and for shading outdoor living areas. Other vines have also been caught up in this wave of popularity. Aesthetically, vines trained up a trellis or post and allowed to spread out on an arbor or other horizontal framework become manmade trees. There is nothing quite so refreshing on a summer day as cooling shadows cast by vines.

Some annual vines are so fast-growing that they can provide a large, dense screen in less than one season, all for the price of a packet of seeds. This is important in our mobile nation, a country where nearly half of us move once every five years.

Contemporary architecture, with its extensive areas of unadorned wall and simple window casements, frequently employs a wall projecting from the house to protect a patio or to extend the horizontal lines of the building. Vines are needed on some of these plain wall surfaces to ornament without smothering them. For this purpose, we have come to think of the tailored vine, a vine so thinned and trained that it is important for the line of trunk or stems and individual leaves, not as a massive drapery. Both landscape architect and amateur gardener will find that vines provide wonderful material to accent or, when necessary, to conceal architectural lines.

Fences and vines go together, and as a nation that is becoming more aware of the values of privacy, we are putting up more fences every year. Vines can serve to complete the picture—to clothe the bare wire chain-link fence, or to break the monotony of wood paneling.

The spacious property of another age has given way to one of much smaller dimensions. Conversely, houses tend to sprawl, and garage areas are becoming wider and wider. Garden space has become limited, so that what is left deserves more careful attention. Vines are one answer because they require so little ground.

The garden of limited space, especially the terrace, patio or other outdoor area, calls for container gardening. This allows plants to be moved to any desired location when they are at perfection. Yet they can be grown in an out-of-the-way place at other times. Annual vines are particularly suited to this kind of culture.

VINES AS OBJECTS OF ART

We have become a nation of gardeners more and more conscious of leaf patterns, plant textures and other fine details. More leisure time, greater attention to the arts and modern methods of disseminating information have all contributed to this awareness. Larger and larger glass surfaces in our homes have brought the outdoors closer to us, and we are more aware of plants. Vines play an important part in the over-all picture. They are available in great variety, and in leaf patterns that become sources of design. Vines are noted for their great flexibility of form. They can be used to provide a solid mass of foliage or they can easily be trained to furnish an open pattern or screen. In addition, a vine spread out over a large wall space displays the maximum amount of flowering wood. Its stems are fully exposed to the light, so that numerous flower buds are formed. All of this can add up to a rich display of color requiring a minimum of ground space.

VINES TO SHADE AND COOL

Apart from the artistic value of vines, they are without peer for shading porch, terrace or patio. Quick shade may be achieved by a rampant annual vine or by a choice perennial. Besides shading an area, vines exert a cooling influence. A house wall covered by a dark green mantle of foliage will obviously not be as hot in the summertime as a bare wall.

Vines are useful also for screening, disguising and providing wind protection. The screen can be an open one, merely to give the effect of separating one area from another, or it can be a complete barrier that might conceal compost pile or garden work center. Vines are useful also to disguise—to cover a clothesline pole or an old tree stump. Tough vines can be very useful as small-scale windbreaks, especially to shield living space outside the house.

Finally, vines may be cultivated for flowers, fragrance or fruit. For any one or all of these purposes, there are vines suited to nearly every climate and situation.

HOW VINES CLIMB

When you select a vine, have in mind that vines climb by various means—tendrils, adhesive discs, holdfasts and twining stems. The method by which a vine ascends and supports itself determines how you can use it. A vine with holdfasts will cling to cement foundations; a vine with tendrils will

COOL SHADOWS IN AN OLD-FASHIONED GRAPE ARBOR, THE VINES NOW
IN FRUIT.   (*Roche*)

work in and out of a wire-mesh fence. You should know something of the natural qualities of various vines before you decide on a site. A trellis is inadequate for a wisteria but fine for some of the smaller pillar roses. And for good looks, good health is important. Vines are among the most self-sufficient plants, but a little attention to basic culture keeps them handsome, and training and tying are seasonally necessary. The way vines climb, the supports they need and their care are now our concern.

Tendrils

Tendrils are modified stems that twist about any nearby support. The grape climbs by tendrils. Sometimes the leaf-stalk itself acts as a tendril—the clematis uses this device.

Adhesive Discs

These are saucer-like appendages secreting an adhesive resin that firmly attaches them to a surface. Boston ivy climbs by this means.

Rootlike Holdfasts

Aerial rootlets, such as those seen on English ivy and climbing hydrangea, take hold of a roughened surface.

Twining Stems

These are a common means by which plants climb. As the young shoots elongate, they make a rotary motion and encircle a small supporting member. They cannot sweep around a large pole or tree, but they can easily encircle wire or cord. Strangely, some move in one direction while others follow an opposite pattern of movement. This habit is fixed and cannot be altered by man. Some vines that twine or turn clockwise are bittersweet, akebia, Japanese hop and Chinese wisteria. Some that turn counterclockwise are honeysuckle, scarlet runner bean and Japanese wisteria. If you are training a wayward shoot that needs a support, be sure to notice the pattern of movement of established stems and twist the shoot around the support in the proper direction.

Weaving Stems

Some vines, which might be considered shrubs with elongated arching stems, need to be tied to a support to prevent sprawling. Jasmine and climbing roses are examples; they have occasionally been termed "weavers" to describe the pattern achieved when a young shoot grows behind another or behind a wooden support and then extends outward. This kind of plant frequently needs to be hand-guided and tied to make all shoots grow in orderly fashion.

HOW VINES CLIMB

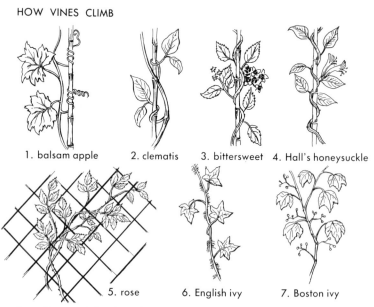

1. balsam apple   2. clematis   3. bittersweet   4. Hall's honeysuckle

5. rose   6. English ivy   7. Boston ivy

1. coiling tendrils. 2. coiling leaf-stalks. 3. twining stems, clockwise.
4. twining stems, counter-clockwise. 5. weaving stems. 6. rootlike hold-fasts. 7. adhesive discs.

FIGURE   7

SUPPORTS FOR VINES

Clinging vines with rootlike holdfasts or adhesive discs on aerial rootlets are best used on stone or brick. Poured concrete walls also are suitable, but the vines may need some wires at 5- to 7-foot intervals to give supplementary support. Clinging vines may be grown on heavy wire fence, tree trunk or tree stump. It is best not to use them against wooden structures because they damage surfaces. Some vines of this type, for example the glossy and bigleaf wintercreepers, develop heavy growth that projects from a building. Heavy winds will tear the upper part of the plant away from a wall unless wires are added to give firm support. A plant growing in the angle of a building or near a downspout is naturally provided with additional support.

All other types of vines may be grown on fences, arbors, trellises or lightweight latticework. Select smaller vines for less sturdy structures. Aluminum trellises, packaged in 8-foot lengths and in various widths ranging from 1 to 3 feet, can easily be shortened by removing one wire of the chain-link or lengthened by combining two pieces. This type of trellis is more appropriate against ranchstyle homes than for larger dwellings of traditional style. A contemporary design lattice trellis may be made with plastic clothesline, using a redwood frame with eyelets or hooks as holders. With these materials, it is possible to create a variety of simple and attractive patterns.

Wooden trellises commercially made for the garden are usually flimsy and tend to be overly ornate. Generally they do not conform to the architecture of houses where they are used. Many of us have found it desirable to have a trellis designed for each particular location. Trellises need to be made of rot-resistant material, such as redwood.

Posts that come into contact with soil are best made of cedar, redwood or cypress. The portion at and below the groundline may be treated with a wood preservative such as Cuprinol, although this is not necessary if heartwood posts of cedar, redwood or cypress are used.

When placing a lattice or trellis against a solid wall, allow at least 6 inches of space between the two. Fasten the framework to hinges at the bottom so that it can be easily laid back to facilitate painting or other maintenance work. Most vine stems are flexible enough to permit this lowering of a trellis. If the vine is perennial and herbaceous, it can be cut to the ground in early spring before new growth has started, the painting done, and the young stems that arise allowed to grow up over the trellis. However, if a woody vine, such as a rose, is to be put on this type of trellis, the trellis definitely needs to have a hinge provided at the bottom. It is then attached to the wall at the top by means of screendoor hooks and eyes.

When wire is used to provide supplemental support for vines, copper is recommended because it is long-lasting, will not rust and weathers quickly to a dark, inconspicuous color. For a masonry structure, aluminum or copper nails can be used, or lead expansion shields may be placed in the wall and screw eyes inserted for holding the wire. Holes for expansion shields may be made with a carbide-tipped masonry drill. See that each hole is just large enough to hold the shield when it is tapped in with a hammer.

Either raffia or jute garden cord is good for tying vines in place. The plastic- or paper-covered commercially prepared ties such as Twist-ems are frequently used and they come in convenient lengths. Do not tie any of these tight. Check at least once a year to be sure they are still loose enough to allow vine stems to enlarge.

OTHER SITES FOR VINES

Pergola, arch and arbor are words often confused, but in this book I have tried to keep their specific meanings. By *arbor* (Figure 8), I have in mind the eggcrate or open framework often placed today above an outdoor living area. This might be attached to the house or set apart at the back of the garden, or it might extend from a garage or other structure. Vines growing on this are trained up on a trellis or on the vertical posts that support the framework, then they are allowed to grow horizontally across the screen to provide dappled shade. The grapevine excels in this use.

The *arch* or *pergola* (Figure 8) is an arched trellis or other type of frame used over a walkway leading from one area to another. Traditionally, this is covered by a climbing rose.

A *treillage* (Figure 8) is in the strictest sense a grill, latticework, trellis or other frame on which vines, trees or shrubs are trained. In describing a vine suitable for treillage work, I have had in mind the tailoring discussed later in this chapter.

Posts, such as the lamp-post (Figure 8) at the front of a property or utility pole in the back yard are important sites for vines.

Tripods (Figure 8), three or more small stakes of wood or bamboo placed tepee style in the garden wherever an accent vine is desired, make good supports for some vines. Melons, cucumbers, ornamental gourds, tomatoes and certain annual flowering vines are often trained on this kind of frame.

Any vine recommended for *container* culture may be used in a large hanging basket, a pot placed on a shelf, wall or pedestal from which the stems can cascade, or in a container to which a trellis has been added. Beside the annual and hardy perennial vines discussed in this book, there are tropicals that cannot be cultivated through the whole year outdoors in the North but that could be used outdoors in summer and wintered indoors in a warm place. These include antigonon, asarina, fatshedera, plumbago, solandra and countless others.

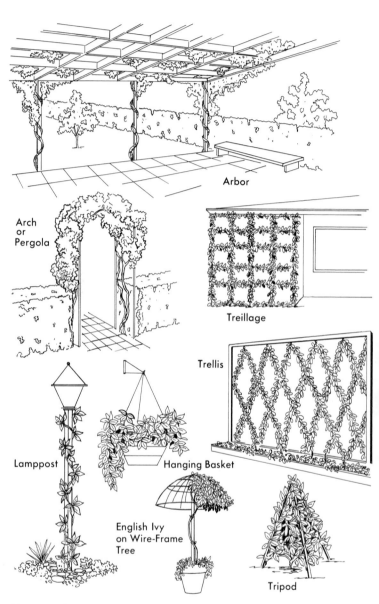

Arbor

Arch or Pergola

Treillage

Trellis

Lamppost

Hanging Basket

English Ivy on Wire-Frame Tree

Tripod

Figure 8

GOOD HEALTH FOR GOOD LOOKS

Vines, like other plants, depend on a suitably moist soil, sufficient light or sun and agreeable temperatures to develop properly. To become superior plants, they also need a certain amount of training, feeding and protection.

The training of vines consists of pinching out unwanted new growth throughout the season, and of pruning old, diseased, broken or undesirable growth in winter or after flowering in spring. A sharp knife and a pair of hand shears or pruners are the only tools you need.

Keep the stems of vines in the pattern or location where they belong. It is sometimes necessary to tie them there with raffia or jute cord or a commercial tie like Twist-ems. The important thing is to make a square or reef knot (Figure 3) loose enough for the stem to enlarge. Check all ties at least once a year to be sure they leave room for expansion.

Feeding and Protection

Vines fed regularly give the most satisfactory results. Practices vary according to the kind of plant.

Most vines are quite free of insects and disease. However, at certain seasons aphids may appear, especially on roses and nasturtiums. Try to check aphids early before there is an appreciable build-up. Malathion is a good remedy. Japanese beetles show a partiality for some vines—grapes, Boston ivy and the turquoise vine. A protective spraying with methoxychlor will control them.

Occasionally when a vine is being grown toward the northern limits of its cold hardiness, you can get it through the winter by removing it from the trellis and laying it on the ground as described in Chapter 10 under *Rosa* 'Climbing Hybrid.'

THE TAILORED VINE

Some vines grow so neatly that they are suited to training into formal espalier patterns or into tailored free-form designs. English ivy is an excellent example. It can be trained into beautiful cordons, into garlands along the top of a garden wall or as an open screen.

Other vines that may be tailored into formal patterns include common wintercreeper (*Euonymus fortunei radicans*), bigleaf wintercreeper (*Euonymus fortunei vegetus*), scarlet kadsura (*Kadsura japonica*) and Low's ivy (*Parthenocissus tricuspidata lowi*).

Euonymus fortunei radicans, THE COMMON WINTERCREEPER, USED AS A TAILORED VINE ON BRICK WALL.   (*Larry Nicholson*)

Support vines in formal espalier patterns by wire kept taut with turnbuckles. For example, to screen a bedroom or dining terrace place a frame for vines nearby. To make such a frame, embed two short vertical pipes in concrete, add an elbow to each and connect with a 2-inch galvanized pipe. This pipe would thus be in a horizontal position just a few inches above ground, and it can be concealed by a ground-cover planting. Extend copper wires vertically from the eaves of the house or from some other wooden frame to the horizontal pipe. Horizontal or oblique wires may be added to make a pattern. Plant a rooted cutting of English ivy at the base of each wire and train it up by tying at strategic intervals. If side growth appears close to a horizontal wire, wrap it around and tie to the wire. Other side growth (that which appears at a place too distant from the horizontal wire to be trained on it) needs to be clipped off. This kind of vine requires regular shaping, but the result is delightful, and any gardener who is interested in being creative with trained plants will want to try this method.

One of the most striking tailored vines I have seen was English ivy planted along a whitewashed brick garden wall. Wires placed in a zigzag or V-pattern the entire length held the ivy in place. When the ivy reached the top it had been allowed to continue growing until the sprays fell over on the other side. Eventually these became long enough to form garlands, which at first required careful tying together at the ends, but after a period of time they had become completely entwined and self-supporting. This kind of garden decoration is a delight to behold and satisfying to achieve.

VINES FOR FREE-FORM DESIGNS

A free-form design is similar to the informal espalier. Types best suited to this are the more-or-less shrubby vines, such as Chinese actinidia (*Actinidia chinensis*), bigleaf wintercreeper (*Euonymus fortunei vegetus*) and climbing hydrangea (*Hydrangea petiolaris*).

Also suitable are the very small and tailored vines that have holdfasts or adhesive discs, such as common wintercreeper (*Euonymus fortunei radicans*), English ivy (*Hedera helix*) and Low's ivy (*Parthenocissus tricuspidata lowi*).

The free-form design may be trained on a small wire or wooden frame or held to a wall—but only when necessary —by the use of electricians' wall nails (not staples) or vine guides. Vines with rootlike holdfasts or adhesive discs are easily trained into free-form shapes when they are planted close to brick, stone or other masonry wall. Maintenance involves only the pruning out of stray growth that interferes with the basic design. A vine so trained makes the smartest effect when kept as small as possible in achieving what is desired. When allowed to grow out of bounds, perhaps to cover the wall, much, if not all, of the charm is lost.

8

Ornamental Vines—
Annual and Perennial

Many excellent vines are predominantly annual or are treated as annuals in the North; that is, they are started from seed each year, they produce flowers and seeds during the first growing season, then die. A biennial takes two years to complete its life cycle. The first year it produces foliage, the second year flowers and seeds, then it dies. The only biennial included in this book is *Adlumia fungosa*. A perennial is a plant that lasts for many years, coming up from the old roots each spring, or sprouting anew from woody stems.

THE ANNUAL VINES

Annual vines are showy over a long period of time and during that part of the year when we are most likely to be outdoors. They may be used as a temporary screen by people who have recently moved, or to give an immediate effect in some area where a woody vine has just been planted for future permanency. Annual vines also lend themselves to container gardening and when handled in this manner, they can satisfy many needs.

Vines grown in containers outdoors need perfect drainage so that excess water, as from prolonged rainfall, will not displace oxygen needed by roots. Dryness also can kill plants, but when dry, they quickly show distress signals in the form of wilted leaves. Such plants recover if roots and leaves are watered immediately and plants are placed in the shade for a few hours.

To plant a container, first be sure there is a large drainage hole in the bottom. Then spread several inches of pebbles. Use a soil mixture of equal parts sand, peatmoss and garden loam. This can absorb water quickly, and yet be well-drained. Apply a well-balanced liquid fertilizer about every two weeks throughout the growing season. The gardener accustomed to standard feeding methods may think this is too frequent. However, rains and regular watering leach out nutrients from containers at a rapid rate. Also, plant roots are restricted and have little space in which to search for food. Mild applications of liquid fertilizer given often should maintain sturdy, constant growth.

As a rule, annual vines or climbers need a lengthy season of warmth and sunlight in order to reach maturity. In northern gardens, start them early indoors in a moderately warm, sunny place, about eight weeks before the last frost-free days in the area. Furthermore, most annual vines do not transplant well. Therefore it is best to put two or three seeds in each 4-inch peat pot. Then when planting-out time comes, pot and all can be planted in moist soil, with no root disturbance at all.

Here are some general rules for planting annual vines outdoors. (1) Plant out only after soil is thoroughly warm and there is no danger of frost. (2) Prepare soil well, working it ten inches deep and incorporating sand if it is heavy clay. Cover twice the depth of their smallest dimension, or with the amount of soil recommended on the packet. (3) After planting, keep soil nicely moist, especially while seeds are germinating and seedlings are young. (4) Install a support at the same time you plant seeds. Then young plants will

A WELL-GROWN WISTERIA IN FULL BLOOM MAKES AN UNFORGETTABLE SIGHT. HERE THE FRAGRANT BLOOMS DRAPE THE ENTRYWAY OF A HOME.   (*Roche*)

never sprawl on the ground and so are off to an immediate good start.

The annual vines discussed in Chapter 10 include bryonopsis, calonyction, cardiospermum, cobaea, cucurbita, cymbalaria, dolichos, humulus, ipomoea, lathyrus, momordica, phaseolus, quamoclit, thunbergia, and tropaeolum.

THE PERENNIAL VINES

Perennial vines are not demanding and for this reason they have often been allowed to shift for themselves, receiving little attention at planting time or thereafter. If they have a reputation for growing too rampantly, it is perhaps more the fault of gardeners than of the plants themselves. These vines usually grow well, but they are more enjoyable if you apply a guiding and restraining hand and use pruning shears wisely.

Perennial vines do not lend themselves to being moved after they get big. Nurseries have difficulty in handling anything more advanced than two-year-olds, and, further, you always have trouble training long streamers on a woody vine to make them look natural. It is fortunate that vines grow fast, so that starting with small plants does not mean you have a long wait.

Be generous in preparation of the planting hole, particularly if a vine is to be placed near a building. If your house is new, be sure that fill placed next to it does not contain debris, such as plaster, chunks of cement, broken bricks and odd pieces of wood. These are detrimental to plant growth. When a house is built, extra drainage is often added at the base of the foundation, and this also may tend to retard growth of a plant set directly above it. To offset these possibilities, dig a pit about 2 feet into the ground with a top opening of about 3 by 3 feet. Fill this with a mixture of good garden soil, peatmoss and sand. Compost that has been fortified with some commercial fertilizer is also excellent. When you make such preparation, your vine will be off to a good start. Be sure to give ample water every week throughout the growing season for the first two years. Also, remember that a vine placed beneath the wide overhang of a house may not receive normal rainfall and so will need additional watering.

Generally only one vine is planted on one side of a house. Near a wall or fence, however, if several plants are needed for complete coverage, they may be spaced about 5 feet apart. Slow-growing vines, such as the bigleaf wintercreeper, might be set at half that distance, and those that grow fast and vigorously, such as actinidia or wisteria, 10 feet apart.

Vines grown for foliage may be pruned at any time. This is especially true of restrictive pruning, that is, heading back to maintain an orderly appearance. When elongated shoots without side branches appear on new vines, they should be pinched back to encourage branching. Remove dead wood as soon as it is discovered. Long sucker shoots should also be removed or headed back immediately. If major thinning-out

English Ivy on Both Sides of Wall

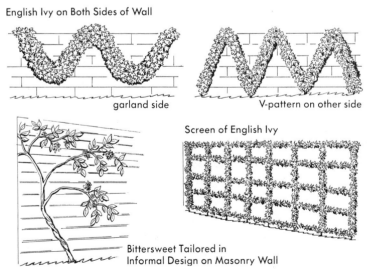

garland side

V-pattern on other side

Screen of English Ivy

Bittersweet Tailored in
Informal Design on Masonry Wall

FIGURE 9

is contemplated, late winter and early spring are the best times.

Prune vines that blossom in spring immediately after they have flowered, those that bloom in summer and autumn early the next spring. If spring-flowering vines were to be pruned early, their flower buds, formed the previous summer, would be destroyed.

Essentially, woody vines are pruned once a year, but this pruning may be supplemented with light snipping and pinching as needed for guidance and complete control.

If a vine has become excessively overgrown and you plan to cut it to the ground, do this when the plant is dormant, not in summer, because any new wood coming from the roots at that time would be weak and subject to winterkill. Severe pruning is not recommended for wisteria since the renewal growth would be purely vegetative and flower buds would not be developed for several years. Wisteria is particularly sensitive and requires a proper balance of root, leaf and rate of growth before it will initiate flower buds.

WOODY AND HERBACEOUS VINES

In Chapter 10, where all types of vines are discussed, the descriptions in Section 2 indicate whether each is annual, perennial or woody. Woody branches persist year after year, and they may be covered by evergreen or deciduous foliage. They are therefore described as "evergreen" or "deciduous." The other perennial vines, those termed herbaceous, do not have woody stems and after the first frost, or by the time really cold weather sets in, they will have died to the ground. These need to be cut off at the surface carefully in winter or early spring, but be sure not to damage new growth. A word of caution: Many hybrid clematis have such delicate woody stems that they appear to be dead at the end of winter. However, clematis are tough and, when protected by a house wall, commonly survive sub-zero weather. Therefore, do not cut out the stems of a woody vine until you have given it every chance to show new growth in spring.

For lists of herbaceous and woody vines, see Chapter 10, Section 3.

9

Climbing Vegetables and Grapevines

While this book is devoted for the most part to espaliered and climbing plants for ornamental use, Chapter 6 discusses fruit trees as espaliers, and so it seems logical to include some information about high-quality vegetables that can be grown on trellises or similar supports. These include pole beans, climbing cucumbers, peas and tomatoes. And then there are grapes.

Climbing vines do well on wire fences or simple lath supports, or on screens made of sturdy cord. In addition to the fact that vegetables grown vertically save ground space, they also reach maturity in perfect condition without being spattered with mud or subjected to overly moist ground conditions. When well-grown, such vines are attractive in the landscape. While they do not have spectacular flowers, these vegetables produce appetizing crops and many gardeners will find them interesting to grow.

CLIMBING VEGETABLES

Pole Beans

These beans need a pole or fence up to 8 feet on which to climb. Plant seeds after soil is warm (they won't germinate if soil is still cold). Prepare soil well, and be sure of full sun.

Plant seeds close together, about every 3 inches. Later, after germination occurs, thin so that one plant stands at every 6 inches. Beans benefit from generous feeding both at planting time and later in the season. A general rule is to apply a side dressing of 6–10–4 fertilizer, or one with similar ratio, at the rate of six pounds to every 50 feet of row. As the season progresses and the weather gets warm, much time will be saved if a 2- to 3-inch mulch of dried grass clippings, straw or cocoa-bean hulls is applied, since beans depend on evenly moist soil to keep up production. Provide at least the equivalent of 1 inch of moisture every week in the absence of ample rainfall.

Cucumbers

The cucumber, so often desired by the home gardener but usually too large for his space, is excellent when trained on a trellis. It is of easy cultivation, preferring warm, sunny days, and evenly moist, well-drained soil. Seed catalogs list

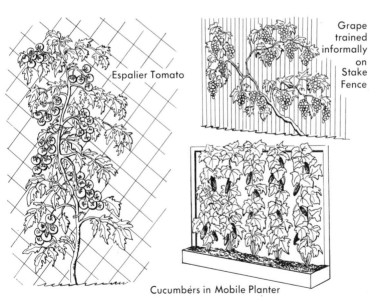

Espalier Tomato

Grape trained informally on Stake Fence

Cucumbers in Mobile Planter

FIGURE 10

many varieties, detailing the outstanding merits of each. The extra-early variety Mandarin is especially suitable for trellis culture. Also, try the lemon cucumber. The fruit is about the shape, color and size of a normal lemon and is considered more digestible than other types of cucumber. These vegetables require a long growing season, and in the North, they need to be started indoors about eight weeks before the date of last killing frost. Sow two or three seeds in each pot; transplant these to the trellis location outdoors after the weather is thoroughly settled.

Peas

Tall-growing types reach 4 to 5 feet and climb well on a trellis made of chicken wire, thin stakes, strings or wire. Peas thrive in cool weather. Therefore, they need to be planted in early spring as soon as the ground can be worked, in a sunny location, with evenly moist, well-drained soil. Space seeds in a row so that they can be thinned to one plant every 3 inches, and cover with about 2 inches of soil. To gain a longer bearing season with a minimum of effort, plant one early, one midseason and one late variety all at the same time.

Tomatoes

This favorite vegetable needs plenty of training to make it grow upright, but extra care pays off in a heavier yield of fruit and a plant of most pleasing appearance. If tomatoes are spaced along a wire fence, for example, a chain-link, with the roots located as close to the base as possible, they can be tied onto the fence and need no other staking. If they are located in an open area, then a sturdy stake is necessary, 1- by 1-inch stock and about 6 feet tall. Pinch out all suckers that form, and tie the stem to the stake every 10 to 12 inches. When the tomato reaches the top of the stake, pinch out the tip.

CONTEMPORARY USE OF GRAPEVINE TRAINED ON HOUSE WALL AND GROWING OUT OF TER- RACE PLANT POCKET MULCHED WITH RIVER- WASHED PEBBLES. (*Jeannette Grossman*)

Tomatoes do best in a temperature range of 60 to 90 degrees F. When temperatures soar to 100 or drop below 60 degrees for extended periods, fruit-set will be poor. Tomatoes are best started indoors at least eight weeks ahead of the frost-free date for your area. Seedmen list many varieties, each with a mouth-watering description. Choose from large-fruited hybrids, cherry-sized midgets or yellow-fruited novelties. A recent introduction from Switzerland, called the espalier tomato, produces long grapelike clusters of fruit that are ornamental besides being fine in salads and for preserves.

CULTURE OF THE GRAPEVINE

Grapevines grow rapidly and, apart from their delectable fruit, are excellent for shading and screening. They are especially welcome as a shade, since leaves do not open fully until the weather is really warm and protection from full sun is desirable. Above or at the side of outdoor living spaces, grapes will make a leafy bower over pergola or arbor, such as an eggcrate-type horizontal framework. For this, vines are trained up in the first and second years; by the third year, there will be sufficient wood to tie and train out into the sun and over the horizontal frame. It is the horizontal growth that produces fruit.

There are various ways to train grapes when they are grown mainly for fruit; probably the most popular is by the Kniffen system. This is a kind of horizontal double cordon that requires support in the form of wire or a thin wooden trellis of redwood. Grapes bear on the current season's growth, so that at the end of winter, excessive twiggy pieces can be pruned out, leaving only the vigorous main framework of the double cordon.

Not all grapes are suited to all climates, but Concord, Niagara and Delaware varieties are widely successful. To learn the kinds recommended specifically for your area, check with your county agricultural agent. The catalogs of some mail-order nurserymen also offer advice on grapes for various climates. General culture for grapes includes exposure to full sun, an evenly moist, well-drained soil, and spraying at the proper times to gain perfect fruit. Your county agent can also help you with the pest-control measures currently recommended for your region.

10

Seventy Excellent Vines— Actinidia to Wisteria

This chapter is divided into three sections: the first explains the terms used; the second describes vines suited to today's gardens; and the third gives lists for landscape use. Study Section 1 to learn the meaning of the descriptive phrases in Section 2. The lists in Section 3 will serve as handy guides in selecting vines for your climate and for any special sites you have.

SECTION 1—BY WAY OF EXPLANATION

Nomenclature, cold hardiness zones, sun or shade requirements, the terms evergreen and deciduous, and flowering time are explained in Section 1 of Chapter 5. The methods by which vines climb—tendrils, adhesive discs, rootlike holdfasts, twining and weaving stems—are explained in Chapter 7. Sites for vines—trellis, fence, pergola, arch, arbor, treillage, post, tripod and container—are discussed in Chapter 7. You can find out "How to Pronounce Plant Names" in Appendix B.

SECTION 2—VINES FOR TODAY'S HOME GARDEN

In the past, vines were often planted solely for their rapid growth. By our standards, most of the old-fashioned vines like Virginia creeper and Japanese honeysuckle were too rampant. They needed a great deal of room in which to develop and, when the allotted space was inadequate, they kept on growing anyway. Such unkempt vines cut off light and smothered other plants. They often concealed good architecture and made jungles of buildings and arbors. Vines with twining habits were permitted to crush latticework and lightweight constructions. As they formed dense masses on wooden buildings, circulation of air ceased, sunlight could not enter, and dampness prevailed. When new shoots were not controlled, vines ran along the ground and were as much out of place as weeds.

Vines for today's gardens are more critically judged. We select on the basis of over-all form and effect. We consider foliage, time of flowering, ornamental fruit, hardiness and resistance to insects and disease. Above all, we are conscious of the rate at which vines grow and their possible ultimate size. There are dwarfs and giants among them, so we can make a good choice for any location.

| ACTINIDIA | *Actinidiaceae* | Bower Actinidia |
| | | Chinese Actinidia |

A. arguta, bower actinidia, from Japan, Korea, and Manchuria, in cultivation since 1874, is a deciduous, twining vine. Height—50 feet. Leaf—dark green, glossy, broad ovate, semileathery, 4½ inches, 3 inches wide, red petiole. Male and female flowers are usually on separate plants; not showy. Fruit—green, olive-size. Sometimes called Tara vine.

CULTURE: Zone 5. Sun or partial shade. Soil—light or heavy, but kept moist through dry seasons. Easily transplanted, fast-growing and may be too rampant for most locations. Rarely troubled by pests. Grows well under city and seaside conditons.

USES: This dark green vine requires a large space and some supplemental support. It is especially useful on brick or stone buildings, for covering walls, fences, arbors or large trellises.

A. chinensis, the Chinese actinidia, introduced in 1900 from China, is a dense, deciduous, twining vine. Height—30 feet. Leaf—3 to 5 inches long, 3 inches wide, dark green above, white and hairy on the underside. Petiole and stem—red, hairy. Flower—1½ inches in diameter, creamy white, with a showy cluster of yellow stamens, mid-June. Fruit—brown, hairy with green flesh, 2 inches long; edible. Often called Chinese gooseberry, as the fruit is prized by Orientals.

CULTURE: Zone 7. See *A. arguta.*

USES: The same as *A. arguta,* except this species is not as large.

ADLUMIA   *Fumariaceae*   Climbing Fumitory

A. fungosa, from Ontario to Michigan and south to North Carolina, is a biennial vine, climbing by young leaf stalks that act as tendrils. Height—25 feet. Leaf—three leaflets, small and thin, give a delicate, ferny effect. Flowers—white or purplish in a pendulous panicle. Individual flowers are similar in shape to those of the bleeding heart, a related plant. Sometimes called Allegheny vine or mountain fringe, and formerly listed as *A. cirrhosa.*

CULTURE: Partial shade. Soil—light or heavy but well-drained and moist. Protect from wind. Self-sows freely. Seeds sown one spring produce flowers the next year.

USES: In a wild flower garden, allow to scramble over rocks and logs.

AKEBIA   *Berberidaceae*   Five-leaf Akebia

A. quinata, introduced in 1845 from central China to Japan and Korea, is a deciduous vine in the North, evergreen in the South, that climbs by twining stems. Height—15 to 30 feet. Leaf—five dark green leaflets digitately arranged, each

FIVELEAF AKEBIA (*Akebia quinata*) HAS RICH GREEN FOLIAGE AND SMALL STEMS THAT MAKE IT USEFUL IN MANY SITUATIONS, SUCH AS ON A DOWNSPOUT OR SMALL TRELLIS, SCRAMBLING OVER A WALL, OR ON AN ARBOR TO PROVIDE LIGHT SHADE.   (*Roche*)

1½ to 1¾ inches long and up to ⅞-inch wide, notched at the apex. Flowers—fragrant and attractive but not conspicuous from a distance, in pendulous clusters, each bearing two sizes, the female flowers larger than the males. Fruit—long and purple, rarely produced in this country unless the flowers are hand-pollinated, has a distinctive flavor.

CULTURE: Zone 5b. Sun or shade. Soil—humus-like, well-drained and moist. Moderately fast-growing vine that can be cut to the ground in the early spring and develop new growth within a few weeks. From Philadelphia southward it may become wide-spreading unless severely pruned.

USES: This vine's rich green foliage and small stems, which are easily pruned, make it useful, especially in the North. In many situations, such as on a downspout or small trellis, scrambling over a wall, or on an arbor to provide light shade.

| AMPELOPSIS | *Vitaceae* | Monkshood Vine |
| | | Turquoise Berry |

A. aconitifolia, the monkshood vine, from northern China, in cultivation since 1868, is a deciduous vine that climbs by tendrils and twining stems. Height—15 to 20 feet. Leaf—light green, deeply cut and subdivided, 2 to 5 inches across, 1 to 3 inches long. Clusters of bluish fruit ripen to orange-yellow in September. Formerly listed as *Vitis aconitifolia.*

CULTURE: Zone 5b. Sun or partial shade. Soil—light or heavy. Transplants readily and grows moderately fast. Has few pests, but Japanese beetles seem to find it delectable.

USES: Trellis or pillar.

A. brevipedunculata, turquoise berry, in cultivation since 1870 from northeast Asia, is a deciduous vine that climbs by tendrils and twining stems. Height—25 feet. Leaf—3 to 4 inches wide and as long, deeply three- to five-lobed, rugose and medium dark green. Flowers—inconspicuous, but followed by clusters of showy berries that ripen from yellow-green to lavender to turquoise, to blue-black in late August and September. Each is spotted and some look like small robin eggs. May be called Amur or porcelain ampelopsis. Formerly listed both as *A. heterophylla* and *Vitis brevipedunculata.*

CULTURE: Zone 5b. See *A. aconitifolia.*

USES: Trellis or pillar.

| ARISTOLOCHIA | *Aristolochiaceae* | Dutchman's Pipe |

A. durior, native from Pennsylvania to Georgia and west to Kansas, introduced in 1783, is a deciduous, twining vine. Height—30 feet. Leaf—6 to 10 inches long, almost as wide, cordate at the base, dark green above, lighter on the underside. The leaves overlap to form a dense screen. Flower—yellow-green to brown, resembling a small, deeply curved pipe; hidden by the foliage, but children delight in discovering one. Winter twigs are green but displayed in a tangle of stem. Formerly listed as *A. sipho* and *A. macrophylla.*

CULTURE: Zone 4b. Sun. Soil—preferably humus-like and rich, but tolerant of varied conditions. Slow to become established, but once so, it grows rapidly. Rarely troubled by pests, excellent in the city.

USES: This vine tends toward coarseness, but is useful in a large area as on an arbor, or heavy trellis where dense shading or screening is desirable.

BIGNONIA   *Bignoniaceae*   Cross-vine

B. capreolata, native from Virginia and southern Illinois to Florida and westward to Louisiana, in cultivation since 1653, is a broadleaf evergreen vine that climbs by tendrils. Height —50 feet. Leaf—two leaflets on one petiole, varying from 2 to 6 inches long and ½ to 2 inches wide. Flower—orange-red, trumpet-shaped, 2 inches long with a bell top 1½ inches wide, in late May, followed by a flattened pod 6 inches long. Toward the northern limits, this vine is deciduous, and dies to the ground. If a stem is cut through transversely, a cross will be seen, thus the common name.

CULTURE: Zone 7a. Sun or shade. Soil—rich, well-drained, but moist.

USES: A colorful vine for wall, fence or trellis. Some persons in the North grow these vines in large tubs kept in frost-free places during winter.

BOUSSINGAULTIA   *Basellaceae*   Madeira Vine

B. baselloides, from tropical America, has escaped from cultivation in southern Texas and Florida. It is a perennial, tendril twining vine. Height—20 feet. Leaf—2 to 3 inches long, heart-shaped at the base and thick. Flowers—white, in a long cluster, late summer and early fall, with the fragrance of mignonette.

CULTURE: Zone 7. Sun. Soil—rich. In the North, dig the tuber in autumn and store through winter in a frost-free place as if it were a dahlia or gladiolus.

USES: Good vine for quick shade around outside living centers, for example by a porch or on an arbor over terrace or patio. Sometimes used as a tubbed specimen with a trellis and careful training and pruning.

BRYONOPSIS	*Cucurbitaceae*	Marble Vine

B. laciniosa, from Asia, Africa, and the Pacific Islands, is an annual vine that climbs by tendrils. Height—10 feet. Leaf —five-parted, deeply cut, light green. Fruit—¾-inch diameter, green with white and creamy yellow stripes, becoming scarlet as it ripens.

CULTURE: Sun. Soil—rich, and in a warm location, so that the fruit will ripen. Toward the North, start this vine early indoors to give it a long season.

USES: Excellent for temporary effects, for instance to shade a porch or cover an unsightly fence. May be cultivated in a container with a trellis.

CALONYCTION	*Convolvulaceae*	Moonflower

C. aculeatum, from Florida and other tropical areas, is an annual vine in the North, perennial in the South, that climbs by twining stems. Height—30 feet. Leaf—dark green, wide but tapering to 8 inches long. Flower—white to violet, 4 to 6 inches across and fragrant. Sometimes called night-blooming morning glory, because the flowers often open in the evening. Seed catalogs list this vine under various names, including *Ipomoea bona-nox* or Evening Glory, with violet flowers; *I. noctiflora,* with white flowers; *I. mexicana grandiflora alba,* with 4-inch white flowers; Giant White with

6-inch white flowers; and Giant Pink or Northern Light with 5-inch lilac-pink flowers.

CULTURE: Sun. Soil—rich, well-drained and moist. Requires warmth and humidity. In the North, start the seeds early indoors to give them a longer season. After the moon-flower vine is started from seeds, the tuberous roots may be

TRUMPET VINE (*Campsis radicans*) BEGINS TO BLOOM IN MIDSUMMER AND CONTINUES FOR SEVERAL WEEKS. IT GIVES A TROPICAL APPEARANCE.   (*Roche*)

kept over winter by digging in autumn and storing in a frost-free place.

Uses: A good screening vine on a fence, trellis or post.

CAMPSIS   *Bignoniaceae*   Trumpet Vine

C. *radicans,* native from Pennsylvania to Missouri and south to Florida and Texas, in cultivation since 1842, is a deciduous vine that climbs by rootlike holdfasts and twining stems. These form a heavy mass that needs some supplemental support. Height—35 feet. Leaf—medium green, 10 to 18 inches long, with seven to eleven coarsely toothed leaflets. Flowers —trumpet-shaped, orange outside, scarlet inside, beginning in mid-July and continuing over a long period. Formerly called *Tecoma* and still listed frequently as *Bignonia radicans.* C. 'Tagliabuana' (Madame Galen), a hybrid of two species, C. *grandiflora* and C. *radicans,* has a showier flower, but it is not as hardy.

Culture: Zone 4b. Sun. Soil—light or heavy, but always well-drained. Transplants readily, grows rapidly, and therefore needs considerable pruning unless a tangle of stems is not objectionable. Does well near the seaside. Rarely troubled by pests.

Uses: This hardy vine presents a tropical appearance, especially appropriate with Spanish architecture. Also useful on rough surfaces such as stone or brick, but best kept away from wood except for a sturdy arbor. Good on wire fence or trellis, but be prepared to curtail rapid growth by pruning.

CARDIOSPERMUM   *Sapindaceae*   Balloon Vine

C. *halicacabum,* from tropical India, Africa and America, is an annual vine in the North, perennial in the South, that climbs by tendrils. Height—to 10 feet. Leaf—2 to 4 inches long, made up of three leaflets or sometimes three sets of three-parted leaflets; hairy on the upper side. Seedpod— green, like a paper balloon, enclosing black seeds, each of which has a marking that resembles a small white heart, hence the common names "love-in-a-puff" and "heart seed." The seed pods are particularly enjoyed by children.

CULTURE: Sun. Soil—light, moist, well-drained. In the North, start early indoors so that the vines will have plenty of time to mature before frost.

USES: Good on a small trellis, low wire fence, lamp-post or container with trellis. A vine of easy cultivation, delicate in appearance.

CELASTRUS   *Celastraceae*   American Bittersweet

C. scandens, from Canada to South Dakota and New Mexico, in cultivation since 1736, is a deciduous, twining vine Height—35 feet. Leaf—medium green, 3 to 4 inches long, 2 inches wide. Usually, but not always, male and female flowers are borne on different plants so that more than one is needed to assure fruit production. The flowers themselves are insignificant, but the fruit that follows in large, terminal clusters has a light yellow-orange husk that opens to reveal a bright orange fleshy seed at the center. This makes a colorful show beginning in early October and continuing for several weeks. The Chinese bittersweet (C. loeseneri) has dark green foliage and produces fruit in showy clusters. It is not as rampant as American bittersweet. The Oriental bittersweet (C. orbiculatus) was once widely planted because the heavy leaf production provided a good screen. However, it has become a pest in some areas by scrambling over and smothering other plants and has lost popularity.

CULTURE: Zone 4. Sun or shade. Soil—light or heavy Celastrus has a spreading root system not easily transplanted, but grows rapidly once established. Commonly twines around a tree to a considerable height with the fruit stalks on the outermost branches. Rarely troubled by pests.

USES: For a large trellis, or sometimes to hide a downspout or unsightly post (provide some kind of wire trellis for t to climb on). This is usually an aggressive vine, and since more than one plant is needed for fruiting, it is not suitable or small properties.

CLEMATIS *Ranunculaceae* Hybrid Clematis
Pink Anemone Clematis
Sweet Autumn Clematis
Golden Clematis
Scarlet Clematis

Clematis hybrida, the large-flowered hybrids cultivated today, are of garden origin, mostly hybrids of *C. lanuginosa, C. florida, C. viticella, C. texensis, C. jackmani* and *C. lawsoniana.* The first two parents are native to China, the third to Europe, the fourth to the United States, and the last two are themselves of hybrid origin. The hybrids are deciduous vines that climb by twining leaf stems, which act as tendrils. Height—8 to 10 feet. Leaf—dark green, either trifoliate or single, the largest leaflet up to 3½ inches long and 2 inches wide and tapering. Flower—color range includes white, blue, red, pink, purple and combinations; six to eight or more petal-like sepals arranged in a flat spray with a diameter of 6 to 8 inches.

Blooming time varies according to variety but may be from late spring until frost. A cluster of stamens and pistils forms an intricate pattern in the center of each flower, not unlike a crown of jewels. This may be light or dark and frequently contrasts in color with the sepals. The seedhead of numerous recurved tentacles forms a lacy globe, green at first, later opening to a pale brown, feathery mass.

Of all vines, hybrid clematis give the most color for northern gardens. Cut blossoms last as long as ten days and the unique seedhead is of interest. In Europe, more than five hundred hybrids have been listed and new varieties appear frequently on the American scene. However, many of the oldest varieties continue to be today's favorites. As a rule, hybrid clematis are not put on the discard list after a few years, as named varieties of so many garden flowers are.

Through careful selection, it is possible to have clematis in bloom from spring until freezing weather in autumn. Here is a guide to season-long bloom: EARLY SPRING, *C. montana alba, C. montana rubens, C. montana undulata;* LATE SPRING, *C. macropetala,* Markham's Pink, Duchess of Edinburgh, *C. henryi, C. lawsoniana,* Nelly Moser, William Kennett; EARLY SUMMER, *C. jackmani,* Comtesse de Bouchard, Crimson Star, Mme. Edouard Andre, Mrs. Cholmondeley, *C. lanuginosa candida,* Fairy Queen, Prins Hendrik and Ramona; MIDSUMMER, Mme. Baron Veillard, Duchess of Albany, King Edward VII, Huldine, Lady Betty Balfour and Ville de Lyon; LATE SUMMER, *C. tangutica* and Mrs. Robert Brydon; EARLY AUTUMN, *C. paniculata,* and in addition, most of the hybrids that bloomed earlier will give a heavy period of repeat bloom during the cooler days of autumn.

CULTURE: Zone 5. Sun to partial shade, preferably with foliage exposed to full sun, soil kept cool by low ground cover plants or a mulch. Soil—well-drained, fertile and on the alkaline side. If soil is acid, incorporate lime at the time of planting, and annually thereafter. Do not allow clematis to suffer from lack of water. Apply a mild fertilizer in spring, either dry cow manure or bonemeal. Mix dry cow manure with peatmoss and work into the soil by hand so as not to damage the roots; heel up around the base of the plant.

In planting new clematis, set the crown 2 inches below the soil line (only 1 inch in heavy soil). Provide a small bamboo stake for support and use soft cord as a tie. Young stems are brittle and may be broken by pets or heavy wind. Protect with a collar of wire mesh, 6 inches high and 10 inches or less in diameter around the base of the plant, extending 2 inches below the soil surface.

The flowering wood needs at least a half-day of sun for

LARGE-FLOWERED HYBRID CLEMATIS AT ENTRYWAY OF HOUSE PUTS
ON A BREATHTAKING SHOW. OF ALL VINES, HYBRID CLEMATIS GIVE
THE MOST COLOR FOR NORTHERN GARDENS. *(Roche)*

best production of blossoms, but the root area needs to be cool. This may be accomplished by placing the plant on the north side of a low wall, for example. If the vine is trained horizontally on a fence, the plant itself will provide shade for roots. An additional advantage of horizontal training is that vertically trained plants have a tendency to lose foliage at the base, and this detracts from its beauty.

It is necessary to prune clematis, but practice varies according to the season of bloom. Varieties that flower early on old wood, like Duchess of Edinburgh and Nelly Moser, require little pruning. Weak or straggly growth can be cut out in early spring and, if growth is very heavy, one or two older trunks might be removed at the base to encourage new shoots to form. Summer-blooming varieties that flower on new wood like *C. jackmani* and *C. paniculata* may be cut back to within a foot or two of the ground each spring.

Clematis may suffer from wilt, but good cultural conditions help to prevent this disease. Also, it is beneficial to spray the base of the plant and the top about every two weeks throughout the warmer months with a fungicide. If a clematis contracts wilt, cut it below the ground line, burn the entire plant, and spray the area with a fungicide.

USES: Showy for a trellis, fence, wall, post or arch. When provided with a small trellis, some clematis, such as Gypsy Queen, Mme. Edouard Andre and *C. jackmani*, make excellent plants for containers. Results are best if the container can be kept in the shade while the top of the plant reaches up into the sun.

C. montana rubens, the pink anemone clematis, introduced from China, is a deciduous vine that climbs by twining stems with some petioles acting as tendrils. Height—25 feet. Leaf —three- to five-parted, the leaflets narrow and tapering, up to 2 inches long and ½-inch wide, semiglossy and thin. The petiole, young stems and new foliage are reddish in color.

lower—soft pink, 2 inches in diameter, mid-May. Seed-
eads—not as freely produced as on the later-flowering va-
eties, but interesting.

CULTURE: Zone 6b. The top growth of this clematis, par-
icularly the flower buds, is not as hardy as that of the more
ommonly grown kinds. If winter-killed, new foliage will be
roduced, but flowers will not appear until the next year.
)therwise, see culture for the large-flowered hybrid clematis.

USES: Same as large-flowered hybrid clematis.

C. paniculata, the sweet autumn clematis, was brought to
England in 1864 from Japan, and later introduced in 1877
) Parson's Nursery, Long Island, New York. It is deciduous,
emi-evergreen in the South, and climbs by tendril-like leaf-
talks. Height—30 feet. Leaf—trifoliate, the largest leaflet
) 2 inches long, dark green, and held late in the fall. The
tems are slender, supporting a delicate mass of growth.
-lowers—white, and small, but in large panicles and freely
roduced. They occur in late August and September and fill
he air with fragrance. Fluffy seedheads add interest late in
he season. The Virgin's bower (*C. virginiana*), a native of
astern North America, is similar but does not produce as
many flowers or have as good foliage. It grows to 10 feet.

CULTURE: Zone 4. Easily transplanted and grows mod-
rately fast. Tolerant of seaside conditions and is rarely
roubled by pests. Otherwise, see culture for large-flowered
ybrid clematis.

USES: Excellent for screen planting, but also for almost
ny location where a large vine is needed.

C. tangutica, the golden clematis, brought into cultivation
n 1890 from northwestern China, is a deciduous vine that
limbs by twining leaf-stalks which act as tendrils. Height—
) to 10 feet. Leaf—five-parted, deeply cut, medium green,
moderately thin, 2 to 3 inches long and 2 inches wide. The

stems are slender. Flower—yellow, in June, and borne on 4- to 5-inch stem, lantern-shaped with slender, pointed, peta like sepals, 1½ inches long. *C. t. obtusiuscula* has smalle leaflets and flowers of a deeper yellow.

CULTURE: Zone 3. See large-flowered hybrid clematis.

USES: See large-flowered hybrid clematis. Dainty foliag and fluffy seedheads in autumn make this very desirable.

C. texensis, the scarlet clematis, from Texas and in cultiva tion since before 1874, is a deciduous vine that climbs b twining leaf-stalks which act as tendrils. Height—8 fee Leaf—made up of four to eight leaflets, each to 3 inche long, dark green with a bluish gray coating. Flower—brigh scarlet in July, 1 inch long, urn-shaped with a constricte throat on a ribbed stalk 5 to 6 inches long. The petal-lik sepals are thick, so that the flowers last a long time. They ar followed by fluffy seedheads as with other clematis. Fo merly listed as *C. coccinea.*

CULTURE: See large-flowered hybrid clematis.

USES: See large-flowered hybrid clematis. Bright flowe color with distinctive shape and long season of bloom hel to make this vine welcome in most gardens.

COBAEA   *Polemoniaceae*   Cup-and-Saucer Vir

C. scandens, from Mexico, is an annual vine in the Nortl perennial in the South. It climbs by tendrils that form at th end of each compound leaf. Height—10 to 25 feet. Leaf– 4 inches long, made up of four leaflets, the normal end leafle replaced by a tendril. Flower—bell-shaped, 1 to 1⅓ inche across, light violet or greenish purple, with a large "saucei at the base, hence the popular name. Sometimes called pu ple cathedral bells or Mexican ivy.

CULTURE: Sun. Soil—light or rich and humus-like, bu evenly moist and well-drained. Start seeds indoors to assui

THE CUP-AND-SAUCER VINE (*Cobaea scandens*) IS A SHOWY ANNUAL FOR USE ON TRELLIS, FENCE, WALL, LAMP-POST OR IN A CONTAINER.
(*Roche*)

maturity early enough to have the blossoms in warmer months.

USES: For trellis, fence, wall or post. Good also as a container plant. The flowers are decorative in shape and have a pleasing color.

CUCURBITA   *Cucurbitaceae*   Small-fruited Gourd

C. *pepo ovifera,* from the southwestern United States, is an annual vine that climbs by vigorous scrambling growth and tendrils. Height—20 to 40 feet. Leaf—large, variously lobed and light green. Flower—yellow or white, followed by fruit variously colored and shaped. The fruit in an array of forms, colors and markings makes the small-fruited gourd popular for autumn decoration. Mature fruit may be waxed to intensify the color or coated with clear shellac for a high gloss. Gourds so treated will last until early December. The related *Lagenaria* and *Luffa* extend the variety of forms and colors that are available in decorative gourds.

CULTURE: Sun. Soil—sandy loam. Sow the seed as soon as danger of frost has passed. The best fruit is produced if it does not come into contact with soil. Chewing and sucking insects will attack, so that frequent spraying is needed from early until late in the season. When branches are 10 feet long, it is well to cut off the tips to encourage sideshoots where the heaviest fruit production occurs. Since cross-pollination is needed to insure a good crop, locate several plants close to each other.

USES: For large trellis, heavy wire fence, tripod, arbor or around a post. Gourds grow rapidly and are wide-spreading. Because of this and the fact that the foliage is not very decorative, this vine is recommended only where considerable space is available away from the house.

CYMBALARIA   *Scrophulariaceae*   Kenilworth Ivy

C. muralis, is a trailing vine, perennial in the South but treated as an annual in cold climates. Height—5 feet. Leaf —½-inch in diameter, rounded, with five to seven shallow lobes. Flower—lilac-blue, small. The stems root when they come into contact with moist soil. Sometimes called coliseum ivy. Formerly listed as *Linaria cymbalaria.*

CULTURE: Zone 6b. Partial shade. Soil—rich, humus-like, and evenly moist at all times. Generally associated with a moist greenhouse, but may persist outdoors in old stone retaining walls even where the temperature drops to minus 20 degrees F.

USES: Exceedingly fine in outdoor containers, or to cascade from one level of the garden to another when terracing is used. A good ground cover for softening effect near stone or wooden steps.

DIOSCOREA   *Dioscoreaceae*   Cinnamon Vine

D. batatas, from China, is a perennial, twining vine. Height —15 feet to twice that in the South where the season is long. Leaf—2 to 4 inches long, often lobed and tapering, the center lobe being much larger than the two side ones, dark green and shiny. Flowers—small, white, in clusters, with cinnamon fragrance. Sometimes called Chinese yam or Chinese potato.

CULTURE: Zone 7a. Sun or shade. Soil—well-drained with ample moisture. Grows from a large tuber, tender in the North. In cold climates, dig and store the tubers in winter as if they were gladiolus or dahlias. If planted deeply and mulched in autumn, they will survive a considerable amount of freezing.

USES: A fast-growing screen for large trellises, posts, arches or arbors. May be a pest in the deep South.

DOLICHOS   *Leguminosae*   Hyacinth Bean

D. lablab, from the tropics of the Old World, is an annual vine in the North, perennial in the deep South, that climbs by twining stems. Height—15 feet. Leaf—three leaflets, from 2 to 4 inches long, and 2 to 3½ inches wide, dark green with red young stems. Flowers—may be white as in the variety Daylight or purple as in the variety Darkness. Seedpods are velvety and attractive for a long period. Formerly listed as *Lablab vulgaris,* and it is said that at one time someone proposed *Lablab lablab,* undoubtedly a botanical name to end all others.

CULTURE: Sun. Soil—well-drained and evenly moist. Does not like to have roots disturbed by transplanting. When the soil is warm, sow the seeds where they are to grow, or start them in peat pots indoors, and transplant later without disturbing the roots. Considered a delicacy by woodchucks, but generally free of pests.

USES: Fast-growing screen for trellis, fence, arch, arbor or tripod. Nice for shade, as leaves, flowers and fruit are all attractive. Sometimes used inside a home greenhouse to give natural shade for bench plants.

ECCREMOCARPUS	*Bignoniaceae*	Glory Flower

E. scaber, annual in the North, perennial in the tropics, from Chile, climbs by twining stems and tendrils. Height— 12 feet. Leaf—twice compound, oval leaflets to 1 inch long, airy effect. Flowers—widely-lobed, orange-scarlet, in racemes 6 inches long.

CULTURE: Sun. Soil—moist, well-drained. Start seeds indoors early in order to gain a long season in the North.

USES: For large container, hanging basket or low trellis.

EUONYMUS	*Celastraceae*	Glossy Wintercreeper
		Baby Wintercreeper
		Common Wintercreeper
		Bigleaf Wintercreeper

E. fortunei carrierei, the glossy wintercreeper, in cultivation since 1881 from Japan, is a broadleaf evergreen vine that climbs by rootlike holdfasts. Height—40 feet. Leaf—elliptical, 2 inches long, 1 inch wide, dark and glossy. Fruit— scarlet, resembles that of bittersweet but not as heavily produced as on *E. f. vegetus.* Formerly listed as *E. radicans carrierei. E. f. c.* 'Silver Queen' is a variegated form with an irregular margin of creamy white on the leaf. It does not grow as tall as the type, and is most effective in a shaded location.

CULTURE: Zone 5. Sun or shade. Soil—rich, moist, well-drained. At best where summers are cool. If subjected to full sun on the south or west side of a building, scale will be troublesome.

USES: The most vigorous of the wintercreepers. Large plants need a wire or other supplemental support to prevent winds or snows from dislodging them. Especially good on brick or stone. May be allowed to completely cover a wall, or thinned out to give a tailored tracery.

E. fortunei minimus, the baby wintercreeper, introduced in 1893 from Japan, is a broadleaf evergreen vine that climbs by rootlike holdfasts. Not dense except for the lower portion of the plant. Height—3 feet. Leaf—dark green, glossy, ½-inch long, ¼-inch wide. Upper stems are completely covered with leaves, and, as there are no side branches, these give a pleasing green tracery. Formerly listed as *E. radicans minima.* The Kew wintercreeper (*E. f. kewensis*) is similar but has an even smaller leaf and grows about half as tall.

CULTURE: Zone 5. See *E. fortunei carrierei.*

USES: This small vine is without peer in a garden of limited space, especially in combination with statuary or on a low stone wall.

E. fortunei radicans, the common wintercreeper, introduced about 1865 from Japan, is a broadleaf evergreen vine that climbs by rootlike holdfasts. Height—10 to 20 feet. Leaf—dark green, elliptical, 1 inch long. Fruit—similar to bittersweet, but not produced in abundance. Formerly listed as *E. radicans.*

CULTURE: Zone 5. See *E. fortunei carrierei.*

USES: An intermediate form of wintercreeper that will completely cover a low wall. It is more effective when some branches are pruned out, allowing part of the wall to be seen. An excellent tailored vine.

E. fortunei vegetus, the bigleaf wintercreeper, introduced in 1876 from Japan, is a broadleaf evergreen vine that climbs by rootlike holdfasts. Height—25 to 30 feet. Leaf—rounded, about 1½ inches long, thick, leathery, medium light green. Fruit—similar to bittersweet but smaller in size and in large clusters, the berries pinkish red in pale pink husks. Formerly listed as *E. radicans vegetus,* and sometimes called evergreen bittersweet.

CULTURE: Zone 5. See *Euonymus fortunei carrierei.*

USES: For a brick or stone wall, fence or as a tailored vine.

GELSEMIUM   *Loganiaceae*   Carolina Yellow Jessamine

G. sempervirens, brought into cultivation by 1640 and occurring naturally from Virginia to Florida and west to Texas, is a broadleaf evergreen vine that climbs to 25 feet by twining stems. Leaf—3½ inches long, generally narrow, dark green and glossy, turning wine-red in winter. Flower—bright yellow, large, tubular and fragrant, late March and early April.

CULTURE: Zone 7b. Sun or shade. Soil—rich, with a cool root run. Able to withstand seasons of dryness and rarely troubled by pests.

USES: Excellent on trellis, wall, other garden structure or to cover a bank. Gives a generally delicate effect with good foliage and showy flowers.

HEDERA   *Araliaceae*   English Ivy
                                          Baltic Ivy

H. helix, the English ivy, in cultivation since ancient times, and occurring naturally in Asia, Europe and North Africa, is a broadleaf evergreen vine that climbs by rootlike holdfasts. Height—60 to 90 feet. Leaf—3 inches long, 4 inches wide, shallowly three- to five-lobed, heart-shaped at the base, and dark green. When older plants reach the flowering stage, the leaf shape on that portion of the plant changes, becoming larger and often having no lobes. Also, the plant becomes more shrubby and projects a greater distance from the building or other means of support. Flower—greenish and insignificant, followed by ¼-inch blue-black fruit in large clusters that persist for several months. Possibly no other vine has been so widely used in gardens. The shape of the leaf has become a classic as a result of its wide use by sculptors and other artists. There are numerous named varieties and cultivars, some with very small leaves and variously shaped, others in colors ranging from dark green to chartreuse, to golden yellow and silver-white. Most of these do well outdoors in warmer climates, but are better used for indoor pot culture in the North.

CULTURE: Zone 6. Sun or shade. Soil—rich, well-drained and moist. Does well in sun except in the northern limits where winter sun causes defoliation. Grows rapidly once it becomes established and is rarely troubled by pests. A good vine for city gardens.

USES: Brick or stone wall, tree trunk, lamp-post, as a ground cover, for treillage or as a tailored vine.

H. helix baltica, Baltic ivy, is a selection found about 1920 growing at Riga in the upper Baltic (the northern range of its native habitat of Europe) by Alfred Rehder for the Arnold Arboretum. It is a broadleaf evergreen vine that climbs by rootlike holdfasts. Height—40 to 50 feet. Leaf—2 inches long, 3 inches wide, dark green with light veining; like English ivy in general shape. The most commonly used variety of cold-hardy English ivy. Makes a more interesting plant if some of the branches are thinned out so that the entire wall surface is not covered. Two other varieties, 238th Street and *H. h. bulgarica,* the Bulgarian ivy, are also cold-hardy. The larger leaf of Bulgarian ivy appears to distinct advantage on a large masonry wall.

CULTURE: Zone 5b. See *Hedera helix*.
USES: See *Hedera helix*.

HUMULUS   *Moraceae*   Japanese Hop

H. japonicus, from Japan, China and Manchuria, is an annual twining vine. Height—25 to 35 feet. Leaf—6 to 8 inches wide, slightly longer, deeply five- to seven-lobed, bright green and rough. Flower and fruit—not distinctive. *H. j. variegatus* has white-streaked foliage.

CULTURE: Sun or shade. Soil—light or heavy. Will grow in a dry place. Self-sows readily.

USES: Makes a dense cover for fence, trellis or arbor. One of the fastest-growing vines for screening purposes.

HYDRANGEA   *Saxifragaceae*   Climbing Hydrangea

H. petiolaris, introduced in 1865 from Japan and China to Parson's Nursery, Long Island, New York, by Thomas Hogg, is a deciduous vine that climbs by rootlike holdfasts, but may need supplemental support in early years. Height—75 feet. Leaf—dark green, glossy, with finely sawtoothed edges, 4 inches long and 3 inches wide. The shredding bark on mature specimens is interesting. Flowers—white in flat clusters 6 or more inches across with the sterile ray petals at the edge in a set of four, mid-June with some flowering for a month afterwards. The Japanese hydrangea (*Schizophragma hydrangeoides*) is similar, and commonly sold as climbing hydrangea. Its bloom cluster has only one sterile ray flower to a floret and the foliage is coarsely toothed, light green, not glossy.

CULTURE: Zone 5. Partial shade. Soil—rich, moist and well-drained. Transplants readily, is rarely troubled by pests, and will grow in gardens near the seashore.

USES: This is a large vine that has good foliage and interesting flowers. May be used on a wall of brick or stone, or to cover the trunk of a large-branched, arching tree. If used against a tree, a good pocket of soil needs to be provided and extra watering and feeding given until the vine is well established. Useful also as an informal tailored vine.

IPOMOEA *Convolvulaceae* Morning Glory

I. purpurea, from tropical America, is an annual twining vine. Height—10 to 20 feet. Leaf—up to 5 inches long and almost as wide, dark green and heart-shaped. Flower—fun-

THE CLIMBING HYDRANGEA (*H. petiolaris*) IS A VALUABLE DECIDUOUS VINE FOR A LARGE WALL. (*Roche*)

nel-shaped, up to 3 or 4 inches across, opening in the morning while it is cool, most closing by noon. Heavenly Blue is
a named cultivar with sky-blue flowers. Other named varieties include Candy Pink (pure pink), Cheerio (day-bloom-
ing, large flowers, bright scarlet), Flying Saucer (striped
color patterns in blue and white), Pearly Gates (a pure
white flower), Scarlet O'Hara (deep wine-red), Wedding
Bells (rose-lavender) and Tinker Bell's Petticoat (double
flowers in shades of pink, rose, red, blue and pure white).
Formerly listed as *Convolvulus major* and *C. purpureus*.

CULTURE: Sun. Soil—neutral or on the alkaline side,
well-drained. Avoid overly rich soil because it will produce
heavy vegetation but few flowers. Make a notch in each seed
with a file to allow moisture to penetrate quickly and hasten
germination. Although the seeds may be planted outdoors
after the weather is thoroughly warm, in northern climates
start earlier by sowing two or three seeds in each pot (preferably a peat pot of soil) and disturb the roots as little as
possible when transplanting. Train on soft twine or on wire.

USES: Quick cover for fence, wall, arbor or post.

KADSURA   *Magnoliaceae*   Scarlet Kadsura

K. japonica, introduced about 1846 from Japan and Korea,
is a broadleaf evergreen vine that climbs to 15 feet by twining stems. Leaf—dark green, narrow and pointed, 2 to 4
inches long and 1½ inches wide. Flower—inconspicuous,
but followed by a rounded head of scarlet berries in the fall.

CULTURE: Zone 7b. Sun. Soil—rich, well-drained and
evenly moist all season.

USES: A dense vine for fence, wall, trellis, arch, pergola
or post. Good for container gardening.

LATHYRUS   *Leguminosae*   Perennial Pea
                                                     Sweet Pea

L. latifolius, the perennial pea, is a vine from Europe that
climbs by tendrils or may scramble when used as a bank

cover. Height—6 to 10 feet. Leaf—2½ inches long, 1 inch wide, in pairs, light green and sparse, but additional green color is provided by the widely winged stems and petioles. Flowers—pea-shaped, seven to nine in a cluster, usually magenta pink, but available in white, clear rose and bright pink. There is no fragrance. Sometimes called everlasting pea. The long-stemmed flowers make good arrangement material for the house.

CULTURE: Zone 5. Sun. Soil—almost any, even dry. This is one of the hardiest of herbaceous, perennial vines; it is not a refined plant, but it produces an abundance of blossoms over a long period when growing conditions seem impossible.

USES: A good bank cover, but useful also on fences and trellises, or to hide a tree stump.

L. odoratus, the sweet pea, came originally from Italy. This is an annual vine that climbs by tendrils appearing in the leaf clusters. Height—5 to 8 feet. Leaf—compound with leaflets up to 2 inches long, light green. The stem is green and winged. Flowers—typical shape of the pea family (winged butterfly) but larger, up to 2 inches across, sometimes ruffled, in a wide color range, and many are fragrant. Five to seven or even more flowers are clustered on each stem.

Where the sweet pea flourishes it is a prized annual vine. However, in most areas, this is not a casual plant and cannot be considered carefree. It requires almost daily attention while in active growth. Early-flowering strains are the most dependable but different types might be tried to find the one best adapted to local conditions.

CULTURE: Morning sun, but shade during the heat of the day in warmer climates. Soil—rich in humus, well-drained, and evenly moist at all times. Sweet pea seeds need to be sown in early spring in peat pots, preferably indoors.

Prepare the area outdoors for planting in the fall so that plants may be set out early. Incorporate well-rotted manure, decomposed leafmold, or other kinds of humus, and bonemeal. Where fall sowing outdoors is practiced (limited to milder sections of the country and black-seeded varieties) the area needs to be mulched after the ground has frozen to a depth of 2 inches. Use wood or string supports for the plants. Sprinkle the tops lightly with water several times a week to prevent drying and to discourage red-spider. Mulch before warm weather to retain moisture and keep the soil cool. Use a mild, nitrogenous fertilizer after the first blossoms open. Pick the flowers daily to encourage formation of new buds.

Uses: For trellis of cord or wire, or may be grown on brush twigs. Excellent for the home greenhouse.

LONICERA	*Caprifoliaceae*	Henry Honeysuckle
		Hall's Honeysuckle
		Trumpet Honeysuckle

L. henryi, the Henry honeysuckle, introduced in 1908 from western China, is a broadleaf evergreen vine that may be deciduous in severe northern winters. It climbs by twining stems to 15 feet, but does not form a heavy mass. Leaf—medium to dark green, elliptical with tapering points, 2 to 4 inches long, ⅞ to 1⅜ inches wide. When the temperature approaches zero, the leaves roll up into pencil-like forms. Flowers—purplish red, not as attractive as those of most honeysuckles. Fruit—long-lasting, and decorative cluster of blue-black berries.

Culture: Zone 5b. Sun or shade. Soil—rich, moist and well-drained. Easily transplanted, rarely troubled by pests.

Uses: Less rampant and not as dense as most vines. Attractive on an iron railing, low wall, fence, small trellis or as a ground cover.

L. japonica halliana, Hall's honeysuckle, introduced prior to 1860 from eastern Asia, is a semi-evergreen vine in the North, evergreen in the South, that climbs by twining stems. Height —35 feet. Leaf—1¾ inches long, about 1 inch wide, with a rounded point. Flower—trumpet-shaped, white turning creamy yellow with age, very fragrant, appearing first in early June but with scattered blossoming until frost. There is a small crop of black berries. The common Japanese honeysuckle (*L. japonica*) is not as floriferous as Hall's or as widely sold today. The yellownet honeysuckle (*L. j. aureoreticulata*) has a light green leaf, heavily netted with creamy yellow veins, and new stems are red in the spring. It is especially attractive in a partially shaded location and grows to 8 or 10 feet.

CULTURE: Zone 5b. Sun or shade. Soil—light or heavy. Easily transplanted, grows rapidly and is rarely troubled by pests. A vigorous vine, which has become a weedy pest in some areas, especially the middle Atlantic states. Avoid placing it near other plants, as the growth will scramble over less vigorous vegetation, even fairly large trees, and smother it by the heavy blanket of foliage.

USES: *Rampant* ground cover or screen, might be used on a very large arbor for the sake of the fragrance.

L. sempervirens, the trumpet honeysuckle, from Connecticut to Florida and west to Nebraska and Texas, introduced in 1686, is a deciduous vine that climbs by twining stems. Height—50 feet. Leaf—1½ to 2¾ inches long, ¾ to 2 inches wide, glaucous blue-green. Flower—outside it is scarlet, long tubular, yellow inside, mid-June to August, followed by short-lived orange-red berries. *Not nearly as rampant as Hall's honeysuckle.* The Tellmann honeysuckle (*L. tellmanniana*) is a hybrid with deep yellow flowers tinged with red, trumpet-shaped, about 2 inches long. It is a vigorous vine, 35 to 50 feet in height, and does well as far north as Ottawa, Canada.

CULTURE: Zone 4b. Sun to shade. Soil—light or heavy. Sun is needed to produce a quantity of flowers. In some sections this honeysuckle is subject to aphids, which become so numerous that the leaf rolls up with them inside, making control difficult.

USES: For fence, wall, trellis, arbor, pergola or post.

MOMORDICA	*Cucurbitaceae*	Balsam Apple Balsam Pear

M. balsamina, the balsam apple, an annual vine from the Old World tropics, climbs by tendrils. Height—10 feet. Leaf—to 4 inches wide, three to five lobes, each pointed. Flower—small, about 1 inch wide in the male, and smaller in the female, yellow, followed by oval fruits to 2 inches long, warty and scarlet-orange. When these split open at ripening, they reveal several seeds covered by scarlet jelly. *M. charantia,* the balsam pear, is similar in all respects except larger.

CULTURE: Sun. Soil—light, well-drained, and moist. Start seeds early indoors in northern climates so that the plants will have time to reach maturity reasonably early in the summer.

USES: Fast-growing but small vine for wire fence, trellis, tripod or post.

MUEHLENBECKIA	*Polygonaceae*	Wire Vine

M. complexa, introduced in 1842 from New Zealand, is a deciduous twining vine that forms a dense mat. Height—15 to 20 feet. Leaf—⅛- to ¾-inch long, and mostly rounded, thin, and dull green. Stems—slender, wiry and brown, interlacing to form a dense mat. Flower—not showy, is followed by a small white, waxy fruit. Sometimes called maidenhair or necklace vine.

CULTURE: Zone 6. Sun or partial shade. Soil—rich or light, preferably evenly moist but tolerant of drought. Withstands seaside conditions.

USES: The supple stems of this plant and its low cascading habit make it very suitable to cover rocks, on a chimney or against a brick or stone wall.

PARTHENOCISSUS   *Vitaceae*   Boston Ivy
                                            Low's Ivy

P. tricuspidata, the Boston ivy, introduced in 1862 from Japan and central China, is a deciduous vine that climbs by rootlike holdfasts. Height—60 feet. Leaf—trifoliate, 4½ inches long, of equal width, dark green turning bright crimson in fall. The slender new stems cling tightly to brick or stone. Flower—inconspicuous but attractive to large numbers of bees, followed by small blue-black berries that persist well into the winter. Sometimes called Japanese creeper. Formerly listed as *Ampelopsis tricuspidata.* The Veitch ivy (*P. t. veitchi*) has a smaller leaf than the type and may be sold as regular Boston ivy. Virginia creeper (*P. quinquefolia*), sometimes called woodbine or fiveleaf ivy, is native to the eastern United States. Its five-parted leaf, which turns bright red in early fall, is often mistaken for the three-parted leaf of poison ivy, or vice versa.

CULTURE: Zone 5. Sun or shade. Soil—light or heavy. Boston ivy is easily transplanted. Start with two-year-old plants. This is a rapid, vigorous grower that will cover windows and wood trim of a building unless pruned back annually. Does well in city or seaside conditions, and has few pests other than the Japanese beetle.

USES: Excellent to cover large wall surfaces of brick or stone.

P. tricuspidata lowi, Low's ivy, in cultivation by 1908, is a deciduous vine of garden origin that climbs by rootlike holdfasts. Height—6 to 25 feet. Leaf—not much more than 1 inch long, of equal width, five to nine times lobed, the surface rounded and undulating rather than flat. A slow-growing vine. Easily kept as low as 3 feet without detracting from the natural beauty. Sometimes called geranium creeper.

CULTURE: Zone 5b. Thrives in rich, humus-like, well-drained soil, but otherwise requires the same culture as *P. tricuspidata.*

USES: An excellent tailored vine, small leaves. May be used to cover a small space or to form a tracery rather than a mass of foliage on a larger wall. Excellent on low wall.

PASSIFLORA   *Passifloraceae*   Passionflower

P. incarnata, the wild passionflower that occurs from Virginia to Florida and westward to Texas is a perennial, tendril-climbing vine to 20 feet. Leaf—three-lobed and toothed. Flower—2- to 3-inch diameter, white and purplish pink, midsummer to fall. Fruit—yellow, edible, about 1½ inches long. Sometimes called wild apricot vine.

CULTURE: Zone 7. Sun. Soil—light, well-drained and evenly moist. Beyond the cold hardiness range, this passionflower and the many other showy species, varieties and cultivars, may be grown as potted plants, kept indoors in a frost-free place through the winter.

USES: Showy for fence or trellis.

PERIPLOCA   *Asclepiadaceae*   Silk Vine

P. graeca, brought into cultivation in 1597 from southern Europe and western Asia, is a deciduous twining vine. Height—35 to 40 feet. Leaf—very dark green, glossy, mostly narrow and pointed, up to 4 inches in length, and 1 or more inches wide. Flower—1 inch across, greenish yellow outside, brownish purple inside, in June, with unpleasant odor. The seedpod consists of two green stringbean-like pods bowed and usually joined at the bottom as well as at the top. In fall they open to display fluffy seeds similar to those of milkweed. The juice that exudes from broken stems is poisonous to some persons. Suckers may be troublesome.

CULTURE: Zone 6. Sun. Soil—light or heavy. Difficult to transplant, and best started from seed. Grows rapidly, and although the top will die to the ground in the northern limits, it makes a quick comeback, particularly if deeply mulched through winter. Rarely troubled by pests.

USES: Gives a strong silhouette on fence, trellis, wall or arbor. Train branches to spread out rather than intertwine. Thin carefully each spring.

PHASEOLUS   *Leguminosae*   Scarlet Runner Bean

P. coccineus, from the American tropics, is an annual vine in the North, perennial and evergreen in the South, that climbs by tendrils equipped with suction discs. Height—30 to 40 feet. Leaf—compound, made up of two or three leaflets, each 2 to 3 inches long, dark green and shiny. Flowers —deep scarlet, trumpet-shaped, 1 inch long, ten or more in a pendulous cluster, and produced in quantity. Formerly listed as *P. multiflorus.* Sometimes called fire bean.

CULTURE: Sun. Soil—rich, moist, well-drained. Locate in open area where there is good circulation of air. Fast-growing after roots are established and weather becomes warm.

USES: A vigorous vine that grows fast and makes a good screen on fence, arbor, wall or trellis. In warmer areas, do not use it on wooden structures, as the suction discs might cause damage.

POLYGONUM   *Polygonaceae*   Silver Lace Vine

P. auberti, introduced in 1899 from western China, is a deciduous twining vine. Height—25 feet. Leaf—2 inches long, 1½ inches wide, and sparse. Flowers—white and small, produced in panicles 6 to 8 inches long, which give an airy effect when they appear in August and September. Sometimes called Chinese fleece vine.

CULTURE: Zone 5. Sun. Soil—light or heavy. Easily transplanted, grows rapidly, and tolerant of seaside conditions. Thin out in early spring.

USES: For fence, wall, trellis, tree trunk or arbor. This vine flowers in late summer when little else is in bloom, exceptionally good on a heavy wire fence.

PUERARIA	*Leguminosae*	Kudzu Vine

P. thunbergiana, brought into cultivation in 1885 from China and Japan, is a deciduous vine that twines, but not as tightly as most vines. Height—75 feet in the South, about half that in the North. Leaf—made up of three leaflets, each 2½ to 3 inches long, 1½ to 2 inches wide, sometimes lobed, dark green on the upper side, quite hairy beneath. Flowers —purple, pea-shaped, in a wisteria-like cluster, but smaller, in August. The buds are not hardy in the vine's northern limits. Sometimes called Kudzu bean.

CULTURE: Zone 6. Sun. Soil—light and well-drained. The root is tuberous and not easily transplanted. Grows rapidly. Where it flourishes, this vine spreads by underground runners and it has become a pest in some gardens of the South.

USES: Makes a dense screen on fence, wall, trellis or arbor. In warmer sections of the country, this is valued as the fastest-growing vine for screening purposes. A good choice for planting on heavy wire fences.

QUAMOCLIT	*Convolvulaceae*	Cypress Vine Cardinal Climber

Q. pennata, the cypress vine, from Arizona and New Mexico, is an annual vine that climbs by twining stems. Height —10 feet. Leaf—compound, of as many as nineteen very narrow leaflets, extremely dark green, creating a lacy foliage effect. Flower—funnel-shaped with a bell end that forms a perfect star, scarlet, open in the morning and evening but not in the warmest parts of the day.

CULTURE: Sun or partial shade. Soil—light and well-drained. Do not expose to strong winds. Young seedlings need to be tied up while they are becoming established.

USES: A dainty vine, suitable for a lamp-post, lattice or fence, but also for other locations in general, such as a trellis or a container.

Q. sloteri, the cardinal climber, a hybrid between *Q. pennata* and *Q. coccinea* of garden origin, is an annual twining vine. Height—15 feet. Leaf—4 inches wide, deeply lobed into as many as fifteen segments; dark green and glossy. Flower—scarlet with white throat, up to 1½ inches across and 2 inches long. Five to seven in a cluster.

CULTURE: See *Q. pennata*.

USES: See *Q. pennata*.

ROSA	*Rosaceae*	Banks' Rose
		Climbing Hybrid Rose
		Cherokee Rose

R. banksiae, the Banks' rose, from China, is a broadleaf evergreen vinelike shrub. The long branches need to be trained in order to give the effect of a vine, as it is naturally a scrambling plant. Height—40 feet. Leaf—three to five leaflets, 1 to 2½ inches long and about a third as wide. No thorns. Flower—yellow-buff, double, 1½ inches in diameter, many to a cluster, mid-April. A double white form introduced in 1807 is not as common. In the South, this is frequently planted near wisteria, as the flowers make a pleasing combination. The only important rose with evergreen foliage, and it is fragrant.

CULTURE: Zone 7b. Sun. Soil—light or heavy.

USES: A tender vine excellent on a fence, wall, strong trellis or arch, in climates that are mild enough for it.

R. 'Climbing Hybrid,' a term used to describe the many climbing roses in cultivation today, most of which are of garden origin and generally derived from complex crosses using *R. multiflora, R. wichuriana* and *R. setigera.* Some are tall-growing sports of hybrid tea and other bush varieties and cultivars. Basically they are deciduous, scrambling shrubs with long branches that need to be trained and supported to give the effect of vines. Height—10 to 20 feet (6 to 10 feet for pillar types). Leaf—three to nine leaflets, dark green, glossy. Thorny stems. Flowers—mostly double, but some singles are available, varying in size from 2 to 4 inches, and the color range includes white, to yellow, to pink, to deep red and multicolor. Fragrance is present in most. The flowering time is June, and climbing sports of hybrid tea varieties and some others have recurrent or continuous bloom.

The climbing rose is represented by several distinct types with an occasional overlapping. A simplified classification of popular varieties follows. The number in parentheses following each variety name is the national rating given it by the American Rose Society (headquarters are at 4048 Roselea Place, Columbus, Ohio). A rating of 10 represents a perfect score.

EVERBLOOMING LARGE-FLOWERED CLIMBERS

This is the most popular group of climbing roses today. There are numerous flowers in June and early July, some scattered through the summer, and usually an abundance in the cool days of autumn. Good varieties include Blaze (8.1) with scarlet flowers; Don Juan (8.2), dark red; New Dawn (9.8), silvery pink; White Dawn (8.5), white.

LARGE-FLOWERED CLIMBERS

The large-flowered climbers represent an earlier improvement over rambler roses, but they have since largely been replaced by the everblooming group. Varieties: City of York

(8.6), creamy white; Doubloons (7.1), yellow; Dr. Huey (7.3), deep red; Dr. J. H. Nicholas (7.1), medium pink; Dr. W. Van Fleet (8.7), a soft pink largely replaced by the everblooming New Dawn; Paul's Scarlet (9.0), scarlet; Silver Moon (8.0), white.

CLIMBING HYBRID TEAS

These are sports of the bush hybrid tea roses cultivated in gardens everywhere. Flowering continues throughout the normal rose season. Popular in milder climates but generally tender in the North. They have a cold hardiness rating of Zone 7a. Varieties: Climbing Charlotte Armstrong (9.0), light red; Climbing Crimson Glory (8.3), dark red; Climbing Peace (7.2), cream with pink edging; Climbing Sutter's Gold (6.7), yellow blend.

CLIMBING FLORIBUNDAS

Climbing floribundas are sports of popular floribunda bush roses. They flower throughout the normal rose season and are hardier than climbing hybrid teas, but there is not as wide a selection. Recommended varieties include: Climbing Goldilocks (6.7), yellow; Climbing Pinkie (9.0), bright pink; Climbing Summer Snow (7.4), white.

RAMBLERS

Ramblers, hardiest of climbing roses, have clusters of small flowers (2-inch diameter). They are useful on arches because of the pliable stems, and do well near the seaside. In general they have been superseded by the large-flowered varieties. Not always available at local garden center, but obtainable from mail-order specialists in old roses. Two recommended varieties are Chevy Chase (8.9), medium red, and Dorothy Perkins (5.9), light pink.

PILLARS

Pillar roses have stiff, upright stems to 10 feet and they are best trained vertically rather than horizontally. Good varieties include: Don Juan (8.2), dark red; Dream Girl (7.3) pink blend; Golden Showers (7.4), yellow; High Noon (7.9), yellow; Inspiration (7.6), medium pink; Parade (8.1) deep pink.

TRAILING ROSES

These have pliable stems and smaller leaves than other climbing roses. They may be used as a ground cover or allowed to scramble or cascade from a low wall or fence. Two recommended varieties are Max Graf (8.1), pink, and Yellow Creeping Everbloom (7.0), yellow.

CULTURE: Zone 6a (7a for climbing hybrid teas). Sun—at least five hours daily. Soil—light or heavy but well-drained and evenly moist. Prepare planting areas well, incorporating dry or well-rotted cow manure at the bottom of the hole. Be sure there is a 3-inch layer of soil mixed with peatmoss between the manure and the rose roots. Spring planting is advisable in all except very warm sections. In the transition area between warm and cold, fall planting if practiced needs to be accompanied by the mounding of soil around the base of the newly transplanted rose. In general, climbing hybrid roses are not as prone to insect and disease attack as hybrid teas and other bush roses. The most common pests are aphids, red-spider mites and Japanese beetles. Spray every seven to ten days with an all-purpose insecticide-fungicide mixture. Apply a complete fertilizer in early spring and again at the beginning of summer.

The large-flowered climbers require little pruning other than the removal of dead wood and weak shoots in early spring. Any excess of old canes can be cut out at the same time. Branches that become too long can be headed back at ıny time. Pruning encourages new, strong suckers that will)ear heavily the following year. After the plant has bloomed, remove stems that have old flower clusters, cutting back to a section that bears five to seven leaflets. Training portions of canes horizontally produces laterals and therefore more blooms.

Rambler roses are pruned more severely. As soon as the old canes have flowered, most of them are cut to the ground line, leaving the new wood that is already forming and which will bear flowers the following year.

Climbing roses need to be tied to some support, otherwise their long, thorny stems will branch over pathways and give an unkempt appearance to the garden. Tie loosely with soft cord, raffia or a thin plastic- or paper-covered wire, which comes in rolls or cut in various lengths.

In colder climates where the tops are subject to winter injury, the canes of climbing roses need to be laid on the ground and covered with several inches of soil mixed with straw. A deep covering of leaves and marsh hay or evergreen boughs is often sufficient, but with the canes place mouse bait in tin cans laid on sides with both ends removed. The containers keep the bait dry and in a tempting place for rodents.

USES: Climbing roses produce a tremendous number of flowers, many more than floribundas or hybrid tea bush roses. They are best used on fence, arbor, arch or trellis rather than against a building. When they are used against a solid structure, good air circulation is not assured, and spraying becomes a problem. Climbers are more subject to mildew and blackspot if they are allowed to grow thickly into a dense mass where air circulation is poor.

R. *laevigata*, the Cherokee rose, introduced before 1780 from China, has become naturalized from Georgia to Florida and Texas. It is a deciduous vinelike shrub, a scrambling plant that needs to be trained on a support to give the effect of a vine. Height—40 feet. Leaf—three leaflets, glossy and sharply toothed, 1½ to 4 inches long, half as wide and of thick texture. Flower—single, white, 4 inches in diameter, May, delightful fragrance. The state flower of Georgia. The pink Cherokee rose is also highly regarded. *R. laevigata* was formerly listed as *R. cherokeensis* and *R. sinica*.

CULTURE: Zone 7b. See *R. banksiae*.

USES: See *R. banksiae*.

SMILAX   *Liliaceae*   Lanceleaf Greenbrier

S. lanceolata, occurring naturally from Virginia to Florida and west to Texas, was introduced in 1773. It is a broadleaf evergreen vine that climbs by twining. Height—20 to 30 feet. Leaf—2 to 3 inches long, bright green, on a prickly stem. Fruit—dark red. This species is more refined in appearance than other smilax. It is used for decorations in many homes at Christmas time, and frequently shipped north. Sometimes known as Southern smilax.

CULTURE: Zone 7. Sun or shade. Soil—light or heavy. Confine root by a metal rim sunken to ground level, as the underground shoots spread. Seldom bothered by insects or diseases. Tolerates city and seaside conditions.

USES: Makes a dense spiny cover on fence or trellis.

THUNBERGIA   *Acanthaceae*   Black-eyed Susan Vine

T. alata, from tropical Africa, is an annual vine in the North, perennial in the deep South, that climbs by twining stems. Height—5 to 8 feet. Leaf—oval, triangular in shape, to 3 inches long, bright green on long petiole. Slender stem. Flower—funnel-shaped, white to deep yellow, with a deep purple throat. Sometimes called the black-eyed clockvine. *T. gibsoni* is about the same except larger.

CULTURE: Sun. Soil—rich, well-drained, and evenly

moist. Has a tendency to grow downward unless tied to some support. Subject to attack by red-spider mite if the atmosphere is too hot and dry.

Uses: A delicate vine for container gardening, hanging basket, on small trellis, fence or post.

TROPAEOLUM	*Tropaeolaceae*	Nasturtium Canary-Bird Vine

T. majus, the nasturtium, is an annual vine from South America, that climbs by scrambling in long vigorous shoots. Height—3 to 7 feet. Leaf—rounded, light green. Succulent stems. Flower—mostly yellow or orange but sometimes red or white, single or double, up to 2½ inches across, fragrant and produced in abundance. Although the bush-type nasturtium has been more popular in recent years, the vine or spreading types are available from most seedsmen. Bright yellow and orange flowers give a sunny effect wherever used and they make good cutting material.

Culture: Sun. Soil—not too fertile, as a rich growing medium encourages excessive leaf growth at the expense of flowers. This vine grows rapidly. Aphids need to be checked early and often.

Uses: For basket or other container or location where the stems can cascade downward. May also be trained upward on small trellis or wire fence.

T. peregrinum, the canary-bird vine, from Peru and Ecuador, is an annual twiner. Height—10 feet. Leaf—deeply five-lobed, rounded, light green and sparse. Flower—yellow, three-parted and fringed, giving the effect of a tiny bird in flight, a unique, odd formation that gains the admiration of anyone who pauses to observe it closely. Sometimes called canary creeper.

Culture: Partial shade or full morning sun. Soil—rich well-drained, and evenly moist. Protect from strong winds

Uses: For fence, trellis or post or as a container plant, where an open, graceful vine is needed.

VITIS	*Vitaceae*	Fox Grape

V. labrusca, introduced about 1656, and occurring naturally from New England to Georgia westward to Tennessee and southern Indiana, is a deciduous vine that climbs by tendrils to a height of 40 feet. Leaf—three-lobed, each deeply cut, 3 to 6 inches wide and slightly longer, light green. The dull reddish blue fruit appears in clusters, each grape at least ½-inch in diameter, sour and good for jellies and juices.

Culture: Zone 6a. Sun or shade. Soil—light or heavy, but best where there is ample moisture. Transplants readily, grows rapidly and is freer from disease than cultivated grapes. However, the leaves are favored by Japanese beetles. Tolerates seaside conditions.

Uses: Screen on fence, trellis or arbor. The young shoot of the grape with its cut leaves, irregular stem, and gracefully curved tendrils, has long appealed to persons with an artistic appreciation.

WISTERIA	*Leguminosae*	Japanese Wisteria Chinese Wisteria

W. floribunda, the Japanese wisteria, introduced in 1830 from Japan, is a deciduous twining vine of heavy growth. Height—30 to 40 feet. Leaf—compound, 15 inches long with fifteen to nineteen leaflets, dark green. Flowers—violet-blue, in a pendulous cluster, 18 to 36 inches long, in late May before new leaves develop. Individual florets are spaced so that they do not touch and those at the top open first. The seedpod is like a long, green, velvety bean and persists throughout the winter. The Japanese have developed cultivars that have extra long flower clusters.

CULTURE: Zone 5. This wisteria is tolerant of city and seaside conditions. For other culture see *W. sinensis*.

USES: See *W. sinensis*.

JAPANESE WISTERIA (*W. floribunda*) OF VIOLET-BLUE FLOWERS IN LATE MAY. (*Roche*)

W. sinensis, the Chinese wisteria, introduced in 1816 from China, is a deciduous vine of twining heavy growth. Height —40 feet. Leaf—compound, 12 inches long, with nine to thirteen leaflets, dark green. Flowers—violet-blue in pendulous clusters, 6 to 12 inches long, in late May before new leaves develop. Individual florets touch each other and all are open at one time. The seedpod is like a long, green, velvety bean, and persists all winter. This is the most commonly planted wisteria and an old favorite. *W. s. alba*, a white variety, is desirable where the lighter color is needed. It is especially effective against red brick or other dark back grounds.

CULTURE: Zone 5b. Partial shade to full sun. Soil—light or heavy, but not poorly drained. Wisteria has a sprawling root system, and in order for it to become quickly established, start with plants growing in pots. Some plants may be slow to form flower buds and possibly may never do this. Grafted plants or ones that have flowered in the nursery are recommended. Do not fertilize heavily with nitrogen because excessive foliage growth retards the formation of flower buds. Superphosphate applied in a small ring around the trunk of the plant in early summer and worked into the surface will encourage flower-bud formation. Root pruning in early spring will cut down on vegetative growth. To do this, insert a sharp spade 2 to 3 feet from the plant and completely encircle it. At the same time, cut back the top growth at least 2 feet and in mid-July cut the branches again but less severely. With established flowering vines, bloom is increased and neatness preserved by regularly cutting back, about halfway, all the long new shoots in mid-July and again in mid-August. This will slow down vigorous leafy growth. Rarely troubled by pests.

USES: Wisterias are vigorous vines that require a large space. They are best when the upper branches are trained horizontally on stone or brick. Use only on wooden structures of heavy timber, as the thick trunk and wide-spreading twining stems weaken or destroy standard light-weight buildings. Wisterias are excellent on a large arbor. They are sometimes grown in 18- to 24-inch pottery urns to limit the growth and make them useful in small gardens.

SECTION 3—READY REFERENCE LISTS OF VINES

Vines by Height

MEDIUM HERBACEOUS VINES—3 TO 10 FEET

Bryonopsis laciniosa	marble vine
Cardiospermum halicacabum	balloon vine
Cymbalaria muralis	Kenilworth ivy
Lathyrus latifolius	perennial pea
Lathyrus odoratus	sweet pea
Momordica balsamina	balsam apple
Quamoclit pennata	cypress vine
Thunbergia alata	black-eyed Susan vine
Tropaeolum majus	nasturtium
Tropaeolum peregrinum	canary-bird vine

LARGE HERBACEOUS VINES—10 TO 40 FEET

Adlumia fungosa	climbing fumitory
Boussingaultia baselloides	madeira vine
Calonyction aculeatum	moonflower
Cobaea scandens	cup-and-saucer vine
Cucurbita pepo ovifera	small-fruited gourd
Dioscorea batatas	cinnamon vine
Dolichos lablab	hyacinth bean
Humulus japonicus	Japanese hop
Ipomoea purpurea	morning glory
Phaseolus coccineus	scarlet runner bean
Quamoclit sloteri	cardinal climber

SMALL WOODY VINES—2 TO 10 FEET

Clematis 'Large-flowered Hybrid'	large-flowered hybrid clematis
Clematis tangutica	golden clematis
Clematis texensis	scarlet clematis
Euonymus fortunei minimus	baby wintercreeper
Jasminum nudiflorum	winter jasmine

Parthenocissus tricuspidata lowi	Low's ivy
Rosa 'Climbing Hybrid' (Pillar)	climbing hybrid rose

MEDIUM WOODY VINES—10 TO 30 FEET

Actinidia chinensis	Chinese actinidia
Akebia quinata	fiveleaf akebia
Ampelopsis aconitifolia	monkshood vine
Ampelopsis brevipenduncu- lata	turquoise berry
Aristolochia durior	Dutchman's pipe
Clematis montana rubens	pink anemone clematis
Clematis paniculata	sweet autumn clematis
Euonymus fortunei vegetus	bigleaf wintercreeper
Gelsemium sempervirens	Carolina yellow jessamine
Kadsura japonica	scarlet kadsura
Lonicera henryi	Henry honeysuckle
Lonicera sempervirens	trumpet honeysuckle
Muehlenbeckia complexa	wire vine
Parthenocissus tricuspidata lowi	Low's ivy
Passiflora incarnata	passionflower
Polygonum auberti	silver lace vine
Rosa 'Climbing Hybrid'	climbing hybrid rose
Smilax lanceolata	lanceleaf greenbrier

LARGE WOODY VINES—30 TO 70 FEET

Actinidia arguta	bower actinidia
Bignonia capreolata	cross-vine
Campsis radicans	trumpet vine
Celastrus scandens	American bittersweet
Euonymus fortunei carrierei	glossy wintercreeper
Hedera helix	English ivy
Hedera helix baltica	Baltic ivy

Hydrangea petiolaris	climbing hydrangea
Lonicera japonica halliana	Hall's honeysuckle
Parthenocissus tricuspidata	Boston ivy
Periploca graeca	silk vine
Pueraria thunbergiana	Kudzu vine
Rosa banksiae	Banks' rose
Rosa laevigata	Cherokee rose
Vitis labrusca	fox grape
Wisteria floribunda	Japanese wisteria
Wisteria sinensis	Chinese wisteria

Woody Vines Grouped According to Hardiness

Based on 1960 USDA Zone of Hardiness Map: *a* indicates above-average hardiness for the zone; *b* indicates that the plant is more tender than the average for the zone. A perennial woody vine cold-hardy in Zone 3 obviously would be cold-hardy in the balance of the zones given in this book —4 through 7. Therefore the person who lives in Zone 7 may choose from all plants listed, while the person who lives in Zone 3 is limited to only a few. The person who lives in Zone 5 could grow all the plants listed in that zone, plus those in zones 3 or 4, but probably none of those listed under zones 6 and 7. (See page 40 also.)

ZONE 3: −40 TO −30 DEGREES

Clematis tangutica	golden clematis

ZONE 4: −30 TO −20 DEGREES

Aristolochia durior (b)	Dutchman's pipe
Campsis radicans (b)	trumpet vine
Celastrus scandens	American bittersweet
Clematis paniculata	sweet autumn clematis
Clematis texensis (b)	scarlet clematis
Lonicera sempervirens (b)	trumpet honeysuckle

ZONE 5: −20 TO −10 DEGREES

Actinidia arguta	bower actinidia
Akebia quinata (b)	fiveleaf akebia
Ampelopsis aconitifolia (b)	monkshood vine
Amelopsis brevipedunculata (b)	turquoise berry
Clematis 'Large-flowered Hybrid'	large-flowered hybrid clematis
Euonymus fortunei carrierei	glossy wintercreeper
Euonymus fortunei minimus	baby wintercreeper
Euonymus fortunei radicans	common wintercreeper
Euonymus fortunei vegetus	bigleaf wintercreeper
Hedera helix baltica (b)	Baltic ivy
Hydrangea petiolaris	climbing hydrangea
Lonicera henryi (b)	Henry honeysuckle
Lonicera japonica halliana (b)	Hall's honeysuckle
Parthenocissus tricuspidata	Boston ivy
Parthenocissus tricuspidata lowi (b)	Low's ivy
Polygonum auberti	silver lace vine
Wisteria floribunda	Japanese wisteria
Wisteria sinensis (b)	Chinese wisteria

ZONE 6: −10 TO 0 DEGREES

Clematis montana rubens (b)	pink anemone clematis
Hedera helix	English ivy
Jasminum nudiflorum	winter jasmine
Muehlenbeckia complexa	wire vine
Periploca graeca	silk vine
Pueraria thunbergiana	Kudzu vine
Rosa 'Climbing Hybrid' (b)	climbing hybrid rose

Rosa 'Climbing Hybrid' (Pillar) (b)	climbing hybrid rose (pillar)
Vitis labrusca (a)	fox grape

ZONE 7: 0 TO 10 DEGREES

Actinidia chinensis	Chinese actinidia
Bignonia capreolata (a)	cross-vine
Gelsemium sempervirens (b)	Carolina yellow jessamine
Kadsura japonica (b)	scarlet kadsura
Passiflora incarnata	passionflower
Rosa banksiae (b)	Banks' rose
Rosa laevigata (b)	Cherokee rose
Smilax lanceolata	lanceleaf greenbrier

Vines for Special Sites

HERBACEOUS VINES FOR SHADE

Adlumia fungosa	climbing fumitory
Cymbalaria muralis	Kenilworth ivy
Dioscorea batatas	cinnamon vine
Humulus japonicus	Japanese hop

WOODY VINES FOR SHADE

Akebia quinata	fiveleaf akebia
Ampelopsis aconitifolia	monkshood vine
Ampelopsis brevipeduncu-lata	turquoise berry
Bignonia capreolata	cross-vine
Celastrus scandens	American bittersweet
Clematis tangutica	golden clematis
Euonymus fortunei carrierei	glossy wintercreeper
Euonymus fortunei radicans	common wintercreeper
Euonymus fortunei vegetus	bigleaf wintercreeper
Gelsemium sempervirens	Carolina yellow jessamine

Hedera helix	English ivy
Hedera helix baltica	Baltic ivy
Hydrangea petiolaris	climbing hydrangea
Lonicera henryi	Henry honeysuckle
Lonicera japonica halliana	Hall's honeysuckle
Lonicera sempervirens	trumpet honeysuckle
Parthenocissus tricuspidata	Boston ivy
Parthenocissus tricuspidata lowi	Low's ivy
Smilax lanceolata	lanceleaf greenbrier
Vitis labrusca	fox grape

HERBACEOUS VINES FOR SUN

Boussingaultia baselloides	madeira vine
Bryonopsis laciniosa	marble vine
Calonyction aculeatum	moonflower
Cardiospermum halicacabum	balloon vine
Cucurbita pepo ovifera	small-fruited gourd
Dioscorea batatas	cinnamon vine
Dolichos lablab	hyacinth bean
Humulus japonicus	Japanese hop
Ipomoea purpurea	morning glory
Lathyrus latifolius	perennial pea
Lathyrus odoratus	sweet pea
Momordica balsamina	balsam apple
Phaseolus coccineus	scarlet runner bean
Quamoclit pennata	cypress vine
Quamoclit sloteri	cardinal climber
Thunbergi alata	black-eyed Susan vine
Tropaeolum majus	nasturtium
Tropaeolum peregrinum	canary-bird vine

WOODY VINES FOR SUN

Actinidia arguta	bower actinidia
Actinidia chinensis	Chinese actinidia

Akebia quinata	fiveleaf akebia
Ampelopsis aconitifolia	monkshood vine
Ampelopsis brevipedunculata	turquoise berry
Aristolochia durior	Dutchman's pipe
Bignonia capreolata	cross-vine
Campsis radicans	trumpet vine
Celastrus scandens	American bittersweet
Clematis 'Large-flowered Hybrid'	large-flowered hybrid clematis
Clematis montana rubens	pink anemone clematis
Clematis paniculata	sweet autumn clematis
Clematis tangutica	golden clematis
Clematis texensis	scarlet clematis
Euonymus fortunei radicans	common wintercreeper
Gelsemium sempervirens	Carolina yellow jessamine
Jasminum nudiflorum	winter jasmine
Kadsura japonica	scarlet kadsura
Lonicera japonica halliana	Hall's honeysuckle
Lonicera sempervirens	trumpet honeysuckle
Muehlenbeckia complexa	wire vine
Parthenocissus tricuspidata	Boston ivy
Parthenocissus tricuspidata lowi	Low's ivy
Passiflora incarnata	passionflower
Periploca graeca	silk vine
Polygonum auberti	silver lace vine
Pueraria thunbergiana	Kudzu vine
Rosa banksiae	Banks' rose
Rosa 'Climbing Hybrid'	climbing hybrid rose
Rosa laevigata	Cherokee rose
Smilax lanceolata	lanceleaf greenbrier
Vitis labrusca	fox grape
Wisteria floribunda	Japanese wisteria
Wisteria sinensis	Chinese wisteria

Vines and Architecture

Woody Vines for One-Story Buildings

Akebia quinata	fiveleaf akebia
Ampelopsis aconitifolia	monkshood vine
Clematis 'Large-flowered Hybrid'	large-flowered hybrid clematis
Clematis paniculata	sweet autumn clematis
Clematis tangutica	golden clematis
Clematis texensis	scarlet clematis
Euonymus fortunei minimus	baby wintercreeper
Euonymus fortunei radicans	common wintercreeper
Hedera helix	English ivy
Hedera helix baltica	Baltic ivy
Jasminum nudiflorum	winter jasmine
Kadsura japonica	scarlet kadsura
Lonicera henryi	Henry honeysuckle
Lonicera sempervirens	trumpet honeysuckle
Parthenocissus tricuspidata lowi	Low's ivy
Passiflora incarnata	passionflower
Periploca graeca	silk vine

Woody Vines for Multistory Buildings

Actinidia arguta	bower actinidia
Actinidia chinensis	Chinese actinidia
Ampelopsis brevipedunculata	turquoise berry
Bigonia capreolata	cross-vine
Clematis montana rubens	pink anemone clematis
Euonymus fortunei carrierei	glossy wintercreeper
Euonymus fortunei vegetus	bigleaf wintercreeper
Gelsemium sempervirens	Carolina yellow jessamine
Hedera helix	English ivy

Hydrangea petiolaris	climbing hydrangea
Kadsura japonica	scarlet kadsura
Lonicera japonica halliana	Hall's honeysuckle
Parthenocissus tricuspidata	Boston ivy
Smilax lanceolata	lanceleaf greenbrier
Wisteria floribunda	Japanese wisteria
Wisteria sinensis	Chinese wisteria

WOODY VINES FOR CONTEMPORARY STYLES

Actinidia arguta	bower actinidia
Akebia quinata	fiveleaf akebia
Clematis tangutica	golden clematis
Euonymus fortunei minimus	baby wintercreeper
Euonymus fortunei vegetus	bigleaf wintercreeper
Gelsemium sempervirens	Carolina yellow jessamine
Hedera helix	English ivy
Hedera helix baltica	Baltic ivy
Hydrangea petiolaris	climbing hydrangea
Kadsura japonica	scarlet kadsura
Lonicera henryi	Henry honeysuckle
Parthenocissus tricuspidata lowi	Low's ivy
Periploca graeca	silk vine

WOODY VINES FOR THE CITY

Actinidia arguta	bower actinidia
Akebia quinata	fiveleaf akebia
Hedera helix	English ivy
Hedera helix baltica	Baltic ivy
Parthenocissus tricuspidata	Boston ivy
Parthenocissus tricuspidata lowi	Low's ivy
Smilax lanceolata	lanceleaf greenbrier
Wisteria floribunda	Japanese wisteria
Wisteria sinensis	Chinese wisteria

WOODY VINES FOR THE SEASIDE

Actinidia arguta	bower actinidia
Campsis radicans	trumpet vine
Clematis montana rubens	pink anemone clematis
Clematis paniculata	sweet autumn clematis
Hydrangea petiolaris	climbing hydrangea
Muehlenbeckia complexa	wire vine
Parthenocissus tricuspidata	Boston ivy
Parthenocissus tricuspidata lowi	Low's ivy
Polygonum auberti	silver lace vine
Rosa 'Climbing Hybrid'	climbing hybrid rose
Smilax lanceolata	lanceleaf greenbrier
Vitis labrusca	fox grape
Wisteria floribunda	Japanese wisteria
Wisteria sinensis	Chinese wisteria

Vines for Special Effects

ANNUAL VINES FOR FOLIAGE

Calonyction aculeatum	moonflower
Cymbalaria muralis	Kenilworth ivy
Dolichos lablab	hyacinth bean
Momordica balsamina	balsam apple
Phaeseolus coccineus	scarlet runner bean
Quamoclit pennata	cypress vine
Quamoclit sloteri	cardinal climber
Tropaeolum majus	nasturtium

PERENNIAL HERBACEOUS VINES FOR FOLIAGE

Adlumia fungosa (biennial)	climbing fumitory
Dioscorea batatas	cinnamon vine

ANNUAL VINES FOR FLOWERS

Calonyction aculeatum	moonflower
Cobaea scandens	cup-and-saucer vine

Dolichos lablab	hyacinth bean
Ipomoea purpurea	morning glory
Lathyrus odoratus	sweet pea
Phaseolus coccineus	scarlet runner bean
Quamoclit pennata	cypress vine
Quamoclit sloteri	cardinal climber
Thunbergia alata	black-eyed Susan vine
Tropaeolum majus	nasturtium
Tropaeolum peregrinum	canary-bird vine

PERENNIAL HERBACEOUS VINES FOR FLOWERS

Boussingaultia baselloides	madeira vine
Lathyrus latifolius	perennial pea

ANNUAL VINES FOR FRUITS

Bryonopsis laciniosa	marble vine
Cardiospermum halicacabum	balloon vine
Cucurbita pepo ovifera	small-fruited gourd
Momordica balsamina	balsam apple
Momordica charantia	balsam pear

WOODY VINES FOR SUMMER FOLIAGE

Actinidia arguta	bower actinidia
Actinidia chinensis	Chinese actinidia
Akebia quinata	fiveleaf akebia
Ampelopsis aconitifolia	monkshood vine
Campsis radicans	trumpet vine
Clematis montana rubens	pink anemone clematis
Clematis paniculata	sweet autumn clematis
Clematis tangutica	golden clematis
Euonymus fortunei carrierei	glossy wintercreeper
Euonymus fortunei minimus	baby wintercreeper
Euonymus fortunei radicans	common wintercreeper

Euonymus fortunei vegetus	bigleaf wintercreeper
Gelsemium sempervirens	Carolina yellow jessamine
Hedera helix	English ivy
Hedera helix baltica	Baltic ivy
Kadsura japonica	scarlet kadsura
Lonicera henryi	Henry honeysuckle
Muehlenbeckia complexa	wire vine
Parthenocissus tricuspidata	Boston ivy
Periploca graeca	silk vine
Smilax lanceolata	lanceleaf greenbrier
Vitis labrusca	fox grape
Wisteria floribunda	Japanese wisteria
Wisteria sinensis	Chinese wisteria

WOODY VINES FOR AUTUMN COLOR

Parthenocissus tricuspidata	Boston ivy
Parthenocissus tricuspidata lowi	Low's ivy

WOODY VINES FOR SPRING FLOWERS

Bignonia capreolata	cross-vine
Clematis 'Large-flowered Hybrid'	large-flowered hybrid clematis
Clematis montana rubens	pink anemone clematis
Gelsemium sempervirens	Carolina yellow jessamine
Jasminum nudiflorum	winter jasmine
Rosa banksiae	Banks' rose
Rosa laevigata	Cherokee rose
Wisteria floribunda	Japanese wisteria
Wisteria sinensis	Chinese wisteria

WOODY VINES FOR SUMMER FLOWERS

Actinidia chinensis	Chinese actinidia
Campsis radicans	trumpet vine

Clematis 'Large-flowered Hybrid' (also in autumn) — large-flowered hybrid clematis

Clematis paniculata (late summer and autumn) — sweet autumn clematis

Clematis texensis — scarlet clematis

Hydrangea petiolaris — climbing hydrangea

Lonicera japonica halliana — Hall's honeysuckle

Lonicera sempervirens — trumpet honeysuckle

Passiflora incarnata — passionflower

Polygonum auberti — silver lace vine

Rosa 'Climbing Hybrid' — climbing hybrid rose

WOODY VINES FOR FRUITS

Ampelopsis brevipedunculata — turquoise berry

Celastrus scandens — American bittersweet

Clematis 'Large-flowered Hybrid' — large-flowered hybrid clematis

Clematis tangutica — golden clematis

Euonymus fortunei vegetus — bigleaf wintercreeper

Kadsura japonica — scarlet kadsura

Lonicera henryi — Henry honeysuckle

Periploca graeca — silk vine

Vitis labrusca — fox grape

VINES WITH FRAGRANT FLOWERS

Boussingaultia baselloides — madeira vine

Calonyction aculeatum — moonflower

Clematis paniculata — sweet autumn clematis

Dioscorea batatas — cinnamon vine

Gelsemium sempervirens — Carolina yellow jessamine

Lathyrus odoratus — sweet pea

Lonicera japonica halliana — Hall's honeysuckle

Rosa banksiae — Banks' rose

Rosa 'Climbing Hybrid' — climbing hybrid roses

Rosa laevigata	Cherokee rose
Tropaeolum majus	nasturtium
Wisteria sinensis	Chinese wisteria

VINES USUALLY FREE OF INSECTS AND DISEASE

Actinidia arguta	bower actinidia
Actinidia chinensis	Chinese actinidia
Akebia quinata	fiveleaf akebia
Aristolochia durior	Dutchman's pipe
Campsis radicans	trumpet vine
Celastrus scandens	American bittersweet
Clematis paniculata	sweet autumn clematis
Clematis tangutica	golden clematis
Cobaea scandens	cup-and-saucer vine
Dioscorea batatas	cinnamon vine
Dolichos lablab	hyacinth bean
Gelsemium sempervirens	Carolina yellow jessamine
Hedera helix	English ivy
Hedera helix baltica	Baltic ivy
Hydrangea petiolaris	climbing hydrangea
Kadsura japonica	scarlet kadsura
Lathyrus latifolius	perennial pea
Lonicera henryi	Henry honeysuckle
Lonicera japonica halliana	Hall's honeysuckle
Muehlenbeckia complexa	wire vine
Passiflora incarnata	passionflower
Periploca graeca	silk vine
Polygonum auberti	silver lace vine
Pueraria thunbergiana	Kudzu vine
Quamoclit pennata	cypress vine
Quamoclit sloteri	cardinal climber
Smilax lanceolata	lanceleaf greenbrier
Wisteria floribunda	Japanese wisteria
Wisteria sinensis	Chinese wisteria

Appendix A

Controls and Cures for Pests and Disease

Plants that grow upward are apparently more trouble-free than plants near the ground. However, sometimes you may need to control a pest or clean up disease symptoms. If you do, act promptly, following the suggestions given here.

The prevalence of certain insects and diseases varies from one section of the country to another, and even from year to year. Recommended control measures must also be variable at least from one five-year period to the next. This is partly due to the research for more effective controls that is constantly going on. Timing for spray applications is commonly determined by climatic conditions. Since the times given here are based on conditions that prevail in southern New England, an adjustment in the time schedule should be made for other regions. Your county agricultural agent, state agricultural extension specialists or state agricultural experiment station can give you up-to-date information on control measures and also assist you in working out a spray schedule for your locality. Manufacturers' directions should be followed exactly when you mix sprays.

CHEWING INSECTS

Caterpillar, Leaf Skeletonizer, Bag Worm

HOST PLANTS: Most plants are at least subject to attack.

CONTROLS: Sevin, methoxychlor, DDT. Apply as soon as insects appear; repeat applications as needed.

Black Vine Weevil

The black vine weevil grub chews roots; adult weevil eats foliage at night.

HOST PLANT: Yew.

CONTROLS: Chlordane, DDT. Apply as a single spray in late June for light to moderate infestation; for heavy infestation, mid-June and early July. Spray ground with sufficient quantity to soak into soil; also spray foliage.

Japanese Beetle

HOST PLANTS: Foliage of Boston ivy, turquoise berry, rose and grape are favorites. Other foliage plants may be attacked. Summer blossoms, such as the rose, are frequently attacked. Light colored flowers are eaten first.

CONTROLS: Sevin, methoxychlor, DDT. Apply as soon as insects appear; repeat at two-week intervals. Sevin should not be used on Boston ivy.

Borers

HOST PLANTS: Flowering cherry, viburnum, dogwood.

CONTROLS: DDT. Thoroughly cover the trunk and lower branches, and other branches if they are attacked. *Flowering cherry*—Three applications—early July, mid-July and mid-August. *Viburnum*—Prune out affected branches and burn the clippings. *Dogwood*—Three applications, starting in mid-May, at three-week intervals. Do not permit the spray to touch the foliage.

Slugs

HOST PLANT: Clematis.

CONTROLS: Poison pellets containing metaldehyde (sold under various trade names). Apply when injury takes place or somewhat prior to the time the attack usually occurs.

SUCKING INSECTS

Aphids

HOST PLANTS: Honeysuckle, rose, crab apple, nasturtium.

CONTROLS: Malathion, nicotine sulfate, lindane. Apply as soon as insects appear.

Lace Bug

HOST PLANTS: Pyracantha, cotoneaster.

CONTROLS: Sevin, malathion. Apply as soon as insects appear, which often is the last week in May. This pest works on underside of leaf and frequently goes unnoticed until much damage has been done. Repeat the treatment at ten-day intervals as needed.

Red-Spider Mite

HOST PLANTS: Juniper, sweet pea.

CONTROLS: Aramite, ovotran, malathion, kelthane, tedion. Apply about mid-May; repeated treatments are necessary.

Scale (Soft and Hard)

HOST PLANTS: Magnolia, wintercreeper, yew.

CONTROLS: *Magnolia*—Malathion in August or miscible oil as buds swell in spring. *Wintercreeper*—Malathion in early July and again in early September. *Yew*—Malathion in early May or during August.

WILT DISEASE

HOST PLANT: Clematis.

CONTROLS: Pick off and destroy diseased leaves and infested stems. Spray with fermate, maneb, or zineb early in the growing season; repeat several times at two-week intervals.

SCAB DISEASE

HOST PLANT: Pyracantha (fruit).

CONTROLS: Ferbam, thiram. Apply as leaf buds show color in early spring; repeat three times at ten-day intervals.

FIREBLIGHT

HOST PLANT: Cotoneaster.

CONTROLS: Prune out infested branches, cutting well below the blighted region. Agri-strep, zineb as sprays; use these at blossom time.

Appendix B

How to Pronounce Plant Names

acer—AY-ser
aconitifolia—ak-oh-nye-tif-FOH-lee-uh
actinidia—ak-tih-NID-ee-uh
aculeatum—ak-kew-lee-AY-tum
adlumia—ad-LEW-mee-uh
akebia—ak-KEE-bee-uh
alata—al-LAY-tuh
alatus—al-LAY-tus
alba—AL-buh
ampelopsis—am-pel-LOPP-siss
arborescens—ar-bor-RESS-senz
arctostaphylos—ark-toh-STAFF-fill-luss
arguta—ar-GEW-tuh
aristata—ar-riss-TAY-tuh
aristolochia—ar-riss-toh-LOH-kee-uh
atlantica—at-LAN-tih-kuh
atropurureum—at-roh-pur-PEW-ree-um

atrosanguinea—at-roh-san-GWIN-ee-uh
auberti—AW-bert-eye
baccata—bak-KAY-tuh
balsamina—ball-suh-MY-nuh
baltica—BALL-tik-uh
banksiae—BANKS-ih-ee
baselloides—bas-ell-OYD-ees
batatas—ba-TAY-tas
bignonia—big-NO-nee-uh
boussingaultia—boos-sin-GAULT-ee-uh
brevipedunculata—brev-ip-ed-unk-yew-LAY-tuh
bryonopsis—bry-oh-NOP-siss
burfordi—BUR-ford-eye
calonyction—kal-oh-NICK-tee-on
camellia—ka-MEEL-lee-uh
campsis—CAMP-siss
canadensis—kan-ad-DEN-siss
capreolata—kap-ree-oh-LAY-tuh
caragana—kay-ruh-GAY-nuh

cardiospermum—kar-dee-oh-SPUR-mum
carica—ka-RYE-ka
carrierei—kar-rih-EE-ree-eye
cedrus—SED-russ
celastrus—see-LAST-russ
cercis—SER-siss
chaenomeles—kee-NOM-uh-leez
charantia—ka-RANT-ee-uh
chinensis—chin-NEN-siss
clematis—KLEM-at-iss
cobaea—koh-BEE-uh
coccinea—kock-SIN-ee-uh
coccineus—kock-SIN-ee-us
complexa—kom-PLEX-uh
convexa—kon-VEX-uh
cornus—KOR-nuss
cornuta—kor-NEW-tuh
corylus—KOR-ih-luss
cotoneaster—koh-tone-ee-AS-ter
crenata—kree-NAY-tuh
cucurbita—kew-KUR-bit-uh
cuspidata—kuss-pid-AY-tuh
cymbalaria—sim-buh-LAY-ree-uh
dioscorea—dye-oh-skoh-REE-uh
divaricata—dih-vay-rih-KAY-tuh
dolichos—DOL-ik-oss
durior—DEW-ree-or
eccremocarpus—ek-ree-mo-KARP-us
euonymus—yew-ON-ih-muss
ficus—FYE-kuss
floccosa—floh-KOH-suh

floribunda—flor-ih-BUND-uh
forsythia—for-SITH-ee-uh
fortunei—for-TEW-nee-eye
francheti—fran-CHET-eye
fungosa—fun-GO-suh
gelsemium—jell-SEE-mee-um
glauca—GLAU-kuh
graeca—GREE-kuh
grandiflora—grand-if-FLOW-ruh
halicacabum—hal-ik-KACK-uh-bum
halliana—hall-lee-AY-nuh
hedera—HED-er-uh
helix—HE-lix
helleri—HEL-ler-eye
henryi—HEN-ree-eye
hicksi—HICKS-eye
horizontalis—hor-riz-on-TAY-liss
humulus—HEW-mew-luss
hydrangea—hy-DRAIN-jee-uh
ilex—EYE-lex
incarnata—in-kar-NAY-tuh
intermedia—in-ter-MEED-ee-uh
ipomoea—ipp-oh-MEE-uh
japonica—jap-PON-ik-uh
japonicus—jap-PON-ik-us
jasminum—JAZ-min-um
juniperus—jew-NIP-er-us
kadsura—kad-SOOR-uh
koreana—koh-ree-AY-nuh
kousa—KOOZ-uh
lablab—LAB-lab
labrusca—lab-BRUSS-kuh

laburnum—lab-BURN-um

laciniosa—las-in-ee-OH-suh

laevigata—lee-vih-GAY-tuh

lagenaria—laj-en-NAY-ree-uh

lalandi—lay-LAND-eye

lanceolata—lan-see-oh-LAY-tuh

lathyrus—LATH-ihr-us

latifolius—lat-ih-FOH-lee-us

lonicera—lon-NISS-er-uh

lorbergi—LOR-berj-eye

lowi—LOW-eye

magnolia—mag-NO-lee-uh

majus-MAY-juss

malus—MAY-luss

mas—mass

maxima—MAX-ihm-uh

media—MEE-dih-uh

minimus—MIN-ih-muss

momordica—mom-OR-dih-kuh

muehlenbeckia—mew-len-BECK-ih-uh

multiflora—mult-ih-FLOH-ruh

muralis—mew-RAY-liss

nana—NAY-nuh

nudiflorum—new-dif-FLOH-rum

odoratus—oh-dor-RAY-tus

ornatum—or-NAY-tum

palmatum—pal-MAY-tum

paniculata—pan-ik-you-LAY-tuh

parthenocissus—par-the-no-SIS-sus

parviflora—par-vif-FLOH-ruh

passiflora—pass-if-FLOH-ruh

pendula—PEN-dew-luh

pennata—pen-NAY-tuh

pentandra—pen-TAN-druh

pepo ovifera—PEEP-oh oh-VIFF-er-uh

peregrinum—per-egg-GRYE-num

periploca—per-RIP-low-kuh

petiolaris—pet-ee-oh-LAY-riss

phaseolus—fah-SEE-oh-lus

pinus—PYE-nus

plicatum—ply-KAY-tum

plumosa—plew-MO-suh

polygonum—poh-LIG-on-num

poncirus—pon-SYE-russ

prunifolium—prew-nif-FOH-lee-um

prunus—PROON-uss

pueraria—pew-uh-RAY-ree-uh

purpurea—pur-PEW-ree-uh

pyracantha—pye-ruh-KANTH-uh

quamoclit—QUAM-oh-klit

quinata—kwih-NAY-tuh

radicans—RAD-ik-anz

repandens—ruh-PAN-denz

rosa—ROH-zuh

rubens—ROO-benz

salicifolia—sal-iss-if-FOH-lee-uh

sargenti—SAR-jent-eye

scaber—SKAY-ber

scandens—SCAN-denz

sempervirens—sem-per-VYE-renz

serrulata—ser-ru-LAY-tuh

setigera—set-TIJ-er-uh

sieboldi—see-BOLD-eye

sinensis—sye-NEN-siss

sloteri—SLOH-ter-eye

smilax—SMYE-lax

soulangeana—soo-lanj-ee-AY-nuh

spectabilis—spek-TAB-ill-us

stellata—stel-LAY-tuh

stewartia—stew-ART-ee-uh

subhirtella—sub-her-TELL-uh

suspensa—sus-PEN-zuh

tamarix—TAM-uh-rix

tangutica—tang-GEW-tick-uh

taxus—TAX-us

texensis—tex-EN-siss

thunbergia—thun-BERJ-ee-uh

thunbergiana—thun-berj-ee-AY-nuh

tomentosum—toh-men-TOH-zum

tricuspidata—try-kuss-pid-AY-tuh

trifoliata—try-foh-lee-AY-tuh

tropaeolum—troh-PEE-oh-lum

uva-ursi—-YOU-vuh-ERR-see

vegetus—VEJ-et-uss

viburnum—vye-BURN-um

vitis—VYE-tiss

wardi—WARD-eye

watereri—WATT-ter-er-eye

wichuriana—wih-shur-ee-AY-nuh

wisteria—wiss-TEER-ee-uh

Appendix C

Some Sources of Espaliers and Vines

(*Via Catalogs*)

Armstrong Nurseries, Inc., Ontario, Calif. (roses, dwarf peaches)

Bountiful Ridge Nurseries, Princess Anne, Md. (dwarf fruit trees, grapevines and other fruits)

W. Atlee Burpee Co., Hunting Park Ave. at 18th St., Philadelphia 32, Pa. (seeds of vines)

California Nursery Co., Niles, Calif. (roses, citrus, grapes, other trees and shrubs)

Chase Nursery Co., Inc., Chase, Ala. (trees, shrubs and vines)

Conard-Pyle Co., West Grove, Pa. (roses and clematis)

Charles Fiore Nurseries, Inc., Prairie View, Ill. (shrubs and vines) *

James I. George and Son, Inc., Fairport, N.Y. (clematis and other vines)

Girard Nurseries, Geneva, Ohio (shrubs and vines)

Heatherfells Nursery, Sunset Rock Road, Andover, Mass. (trees, shrubs, vines)

Inter-State Nurseries, Hamburg, Iowa (trees, shrubs and vines)

Jackson & Perkins Co., Newark, N.Y. (roses)

Kelly Brothers, Inc., Dansville, N.Y. (roses and vines)

Kelsey Nursery Service, Highlands, N.J. (trees, shrubs and vines)

Henry Leuthardt, Port Chester, N.Y. (espalier-trained fruit trees and hybrid grapes)

Linn County Nurseries, Center Point, Iowa (trees, shrubs and vines)

George W. Park Co., Greenwood, S.C. (seeds of vines)

Princeton Nurseries, Princeton, N.J. (trees, shrubs and vines) *

Scanlon and Associates, 7621 Lewis Road, Olmsted Falls, Ohio (trees)

Stark Brothers, Louisiana, Mo. (dwarf fruit trees, roses and shrubs)

The United States Espalier Nursery Co., Fairwood, Ore. (espalier-trained fruit trees)

Waynesboro Nurseries, Waynesboro, Va. (trees, shrubs, vines, dwarf fruit trees)

Wayside Gardens, Mentor, Ohio (trees, shrubs and vines)

Weston Nurseries, Inc., East Main St., Hopkinton, Mass. (shrubs and vines)

White Flower Farm, Litchfield, Conn. (trees, shrubs and vines)

Will Tillotson's Roses, 802 Brown Valley Road, Watsonville, Calif. (roses)

* *Wholesale only.*

Index

Numbers in boldface type indicate major plant descriptions.
Numbers in italics indicate illustrations.

197

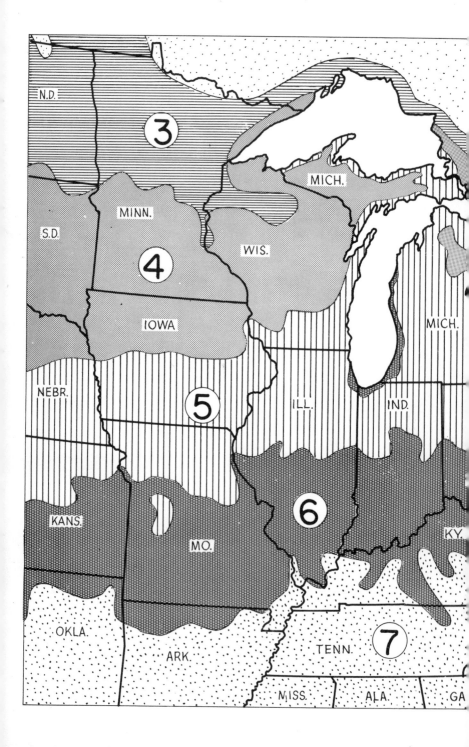